This is an important book for all whose Christianity has become still and sterile. *Fresh Wind, Fresh Fire* signals that God is at work in our day and that he wishes to be at work in our lives.

Dr. Joseph M. Stowell
President, Moody Bible Institute

The Brooklyn Tabernacle is truly following the example of the New Testament church. This deeply moving book calls churches back to the Word of God and prayer and away from the cheap substitutes that are so popular today.

Warren W. Wiersbe
ScripTex, Inc.

Lovingly but forcefully, Jim Cymbala calls us, the Church, to look in the mirror, to repent of all our futile attempts to do the work of the Holy Spirit, and to get back on our knees where we belong. Only then will God supernaturally move to accomplish His plan for our ministries and lives.

Dr. Ron Mehl, Pastor
Beaverton Foursquare Church
Beaverton, Oregon

Jim and Carol Cymbala have to be two of God's most trusted servants. How like God to perform the miracles that have become the Brooklyn Tabernacle, using a kid who grew up in the neighborhood.

Bill and Gloria Gaither

Jim Cymbala's voice is worth everyone hearing. He has a passion and a purity that brings force and clarity to the grand old gospel—bringing it alive with contemporary vitality and beauty.

Jack W. Hayford
The Church on the Way
Van Nuys, California

There are relatively few churches that have a heart for the lost and for the inner city; Jim Cymbala and the Brooklyn Tabernacle are one of the few. They have allowed the Holy Spirit to use them to breathe fresh life into seemingly hopeless lives.

Nicky Cruz
Author of *Run Baby Run* and *Code Blue*

It is without question that God has placed his hand on Pastor Jim Cymbala in the raising up of a great inner-city ministry, the Brooklyn Tabernacle. This church, under his leadership, serves as a model and an inspiration for so many across America. It has been their dependence upon the enabling of the Holy Spirit and the emphasis upon prayer that has brought this about.

Thomas E. Trask
General Superintendent
The General Council of the Assemblies of God

If you ever have the chance to visit Pastor Cymbala's church, do not miss it. If you can't go, you *must* read *Fresh Wind, Fresh Fire*. The remarkable story of this great church and its dynamic Spirit-filled pastor will bring fresh wind and fresh fire into your life.

Bob Briner
President, ProServ Television

FRESH WIND,
FRESH FIRE

Fresh Wind, Fresh Fire

WHAT HAPPENS WHEN GOD'S SPIRIT INVADES THE HEART OF HIS PEOPLE

JIM CYMBALA
PASTOR OF THE BROOKLYN TABERNACLE
WITH DEAN MERRILL

ZondervanPublishingHouse
Grand Rapids, Michigan

A Division of HarperCollinsPublishers

Fresh Wind, Fresh Fire
Copyright © 1997 by Jim Cymbala

Requests for information should be addressed to:

 ZondervanPublishingHouse
Grand Rapids, Michigan 49530

International Trade Paper Edition 0-310-21416-5

Library of Congress Cataloging-in-Publication Data

Cymbala, Jim, 1943—
    Fresh wind, fresh fire : what happens when God's Spirit invades the heart
of his people / Jim Cymbala.
        p.   cm.
    Includes bibliographical references.
    ISBN: 0-310-21188-3
    1. Church.   2. Brooklyn Tabernacle (New York, N.Y).   I. Title.
BV600.2.C86   1997
269—dc21   96-50966
                                                                 CIP

Interior design by Sherri L. Hoffman

Printed in the United States of America

---

99 00 01 02 /DC/ 34 33 32 31 30 29 28 27

CONTENTS

PART 1

Waking Up to a
Powerful Promise

ONE

The Amateurs

I WAS STRUGGLING TOWARD the climax of my none-too-polished sermon that Sunday night back in 1972 when disaster struck. It was both pathetic and laughable all at once.

The Brooklyn Tabernacle—this woeful church that my father-in-law had coaxed me into pastoring—consisted of a shabby two-story building in the middle of a downtown block on Atlantic Avenue. The sanctuary could hold fewer than two hundred people—not that we required anywhere near that much capacity. The ceiling was low, the walls needed paint, the windows were dingy, and the bare wood floor hadn't been sealed in years. But there was no money for such improvements, let alone a luxury such as air-conditioning.

Carol, my faithful wife, was doing her best at the organ to create a worshipful atmosphere as I moved into my invitation, calling the fifteen or so people before me to maybe, just possibly, respond to the point of my message. Someone shifted on a pew to my left, probably not out of conviction as much as weariness, wondering when this young preacher would finally let everybody go home.

C-r-r-a-a-ck!

The pew split and collapsed, dumping five people onto the floor. Gasps and a few groans filled the air. My infant daughter probably thought it was the most exciting moment of her church life so far. I stopped preaching to give the people time to pick themselves up off the floor and replace their lost dignity. All I could think to do was to nervously suggest that they move to another pew that seemed more stable as I tried to finish the meeting.

In fact, this kind of mishap perfectly portrayed my early days in ministry. I didn't know what I was doing. I had not attended Bible college or seminary. I had grown up in Brooklyn in a Ukrainian-Polish family, going to church on Sundays with my parents but never dreaming of becoming a minister.

Basketball was my love, all through high school and then at the U.S. Naval Academy, where I broke the plebe scoring record my first year. Late that year I hurt my back and had to resign from the navy. I resumed college on a full athletic scholarship at the University of Rhode Island, where I was a starter on the basketball team for three years. In my senior year I was captain of the team; we won the Yankee Conference championship and played in the NCAA tournament.

My major was sociology. By then I had begun dating Carol Hutchins, daughter of the man who was my pastor back in junior high and high school. Carol was a gifted organist and pianist even though she had never been formally trained to read or write music. We were married in January 1969 and settled down in a Brooklyn apartment, both getting jobs in the hectic business world of Manhattan. Like many newlyweds, we didn't have a lot of long-term goals; we were just paying bills and enjoying the weekends.

However, Carol's father, the Reverend Clair Hutchins, had been giving me books that piqued my desire for spiritual things. He was more than a local pastor; he made frequent trips overseas to preach evangelistic crusades and teach other pastors. In the States he was the unofficial overseer of a few small, independent churches. By early 1971 he was seriously suggesting that perhaps God wanted us in full-time Christian service.

"There's a church in Newark that needs a pastor," he commented one day. "They're precious people. Why don't you think about quitting your job and stepping out in faith to see what God will do?"

"I'm not qualified," I protested. "Me, a minister? I have no idea how to be a pastor."

He said, "When God calls someone, that's all that really matters. Don't let yourself be afraid."

And before I knew it, there I was, in my late twenties, trying to lead a tiny, all-black church in one of the most difficult mission fields in urban America. Weekdays found me spending hours in the systematic study of God's Word while on Sundays I was "learning" how to convey that Word to people. Carol's musical ability made up for some of my mistakes, and the people were kind enough to pay us a modest salary.

My parents gave us a down payment for a home, and we moved to New Jersey. Somehow we made it through that first year.

DOUBLE DUTY

THEN ONE DAY my father-in-law called from Florida, where he lived, and asked a favor. Would I please go preach four Sunday nights over at the multiracial Brooklyn Tabernacle, another church he supervised? Things had hit an all-time low there, he said. I agreed, little suspecting that this step would forever change my life.

The minute I walked in, I could sense that this church had big problems. The young pastor was discouraged. The meeting began on a hesitant note with just a handful of people. Several more walked in late. The worship style bordered on chaotic; there was little sense of direction. The pastor noticed that a certain man was present—an occasional visitor to the church who sang and accompanied himself on the guitar—and asked him on the spot to come up and render a solo. The man sort of smiled and said no.

"Really, I'm serious," the pastor pleaded. "We'd love to have you sing for us." The man kept resisting. It was terribly awkward. Finally the pastor gave up and continued with congregational singing.

I also remember a woman in the small audience who took it upon herself to lead out with a praise chorus now and then, jumping into the middle of whatever the pastor was trying to lead.

It was certainly odd, but it wasn't my problem. After all, I was just there to help out temporarily. (The thought that I, at that stage of my development as a minister, could help anyone showed how desperate things had become.)

I preached, and then drove home.

After the second week's service, the pastor stunned me by saying, "I've decided to resign from this church and move out of state. Would you please notify your father-in-law?"

I nodded and said little. When I called that week with the news, the question quickly arose as to whether the church should even stay open.

Some years earlier, my mother-in-law had met with other women who were interceding for God to establish a congregation in downtown Brooklyn that would touch people for his glory. That was how this church had actually started—but now all seemed hopeless.

As we discussed what to do, I mentioned something that the pastor had told me. He was sure one of the ushers was helping himself to the offering plate, because the cash never quite seemed to match the amounts written on people's tithing envelopes. No wonder the church's checking account held less than ten dollars.

My father-in-law wasn't ready to give up. "I don't know—I'm not sure God is finished with that place quite yet," he said. "It's a needy part of the city. Let's not throw in the towel too quickly."

"Well, Clair, what are you going to do when the other pastor leaves?" asked his wife, who was listening on their other phone. "I mean, in two weeks ..."

His voice suddenly brightened. "Jim, how about if you pastor both churches for the time being? Just give it a chance and see if it might turn around?" He wasn't kidding; he really meant it.

I didn't know what to say. One thing I was sure of: I didn't have any magic cure-all for what ailed the Brooklyn Tabernacle. Still, my father-in-law's concern was genuine, so I went along with the plan.

Now, instead of being an amateur in one congregation, I could double my pleasure. For the next year, this was my Sunday schedule:

9:00 a.m.	*Leave home in New Jersey and drive alone to Brooklyn.*
10:00 a.m.	*Conduct the morning service by myself.*
11:30 a.m.	*Race back across Manhattan and through the Holland Tunnel to the Newark church, where Carol and the others would have already begun the noon service. Preach the sermon.*
Late afternoon:	*Take Carol and the baby to McDonald's, then head back to Brooklyn for the evening service there.*
Late evening:	*Drive back home to New Jersey, exhausted and usually discouraged.*

Vagrants would wander in occasionally during the meetings in Brooklyn. The attendance dropped to fewer than twenty people because a number of folks quickly decided I was "too regimented" and elected to go elsewhere.

Sunday mornings without Carol were especially difficult. The pianist had mastered only one chorus, "Oh, How I Love Jesus." We sang it every week, sometimes more than once. All other selections led to stumbling and discords. This did not exactly seem like a church on the move.

I shall never forget that first Sunday morning offering: $85. The church's monthly mortgage payment was $232, not to mention the utility bills or having anything left over for a pastoral salary.

I shall never forget that first Sunday morning offering: $85. ❧

When the first mortgage payment rolled around at the end of the month, the checking account showed something like $160 in hand. We were going to default right off the bat. How soon would it take to lose the building and be tossed out into the street? That Monday, my day off, I remember praying, "Lord, you have to help me. I don't know much—but I *do* know that we have to pay this mortgage."

I went to the church on Tuesday. *Well, maybe someone will send some money out of the blue*, I told myself, *like what happened so often with George Mueller and his orphanage back in England—he just prayed, and a letter or a visitor would arrive to meet his need.*

The mail came that day—and there was nothing but bills and fliers.

Now I was trapped. I went upstairs, sat at my little desk, put my head down, and began to cry. "God," I sobbed, "what can I do? We can't even pay the mortgage." That night was the midweek service, and I knew there wouldn't be more than three or four people attending. The offering would probably be less than ten dollars. How was I going to get through this?

I called out to the Lord for a full hour or so. Eventually, I dried my tears—and a new thought came. *Wait a minute! Besides the mail slot in the front door, the church also has a post office box. I'll go across the street and see what's there. Surely God will answer my prayer!*

With renewed confidence I walked across the street, crossed the post office lobby, and twirled the knob on the little box. I peered inside . . .

Nothing.

As I stepped back into the sunshine, trucks roared down Atlantic Avenue. If one had flattened me just then, I wouldn't have felt any lower. Was God abandoning us? Was I doing something that displeased him? I trudged wearily back across the street to the little building.

As I unlocked the door, I was met with another surprise. There on the foyer floor was something that hadn't been there just three minutes earlier: a simple white envelope. No address, no stamp—nothing. Just a white envelope.

With trembling hands I opened it to find . . . *two $50 bills.*

I began shouting all by myself in the empty church. "God, you came through! You came through!" We had $160 in the bank, and with this $100 we could make the mortgage payment. My soul let out a deep "Hallelujah!" What a lesson for a disheartened young pastor!

To this day I don't know where that money came from. I only know it was a sign to me that God was near—and faithful.

BREAKDOWN

THE HECTIC SCHEDULE, of course, was wearing us out, and Carol and I soon realized we should cast our lot with one church or the other. Oddly enough, we began to feel drawn to Brooklyn, even though our only salary came from the Newark church. Remarkably, God put it into both our hearts to commit ourselves, for better or worse, to the fledgling Brooklyn Tabernacle. We somehow knew that was where we belonged.

Both of us quickly took second jobs—she in a school cafeteria, I as a junior high basketball coach. We had no health insurance. Somehow we put food on the table and bought gas for the car, but that was about it.

I didn't know whether this was a normal experience in the ministry or not; I had no preconceived ideas from Bible college or seminary by which to judge, because I hadn't been there. We were just blundering along all by ourselves. Even Carol's father didn't offer a lot of advice or perspective; I guess he thought I would learn more in the school of hard knocks. He often told me, "Jim, you're just going to have to find your own way, under God, of ministering to people."

On one of those Sunday nights early on, I was so depressed by what I saw—and even more by what I felt in my spirit—that I literally could not preach. Five minutes into my sermon, I began choking on the words. Tears filled my eyes. Gloom engulfed me. All I could say to the people was "I'm sorry ... I ... I can't preach in this atmosphere. ... Something is terribly wrong. ... I don't know what to say—I can't go on. ... Carol, would you play something on the piano, and would the rest of you come to this altar? If we don't see God help us, I don't know. ..." With that, I just quit. It was embarrassing, but I couldn't do anything else.

The people did as I asked. I leaned into the pulpit, my face planted in my hands, and sobbed. Things were quiet at first, but soon the Spirit of God came down upon us. People began to call upon the Lord, their words motivated by a stirring within. "God, help us," we prayed. Carol played the old hymn "I Need Thee, Oh, I Need Thee," and we sang along. A tide of intercession arose.

Suddenly a young usher came running down the center aisle and threw himself on the altar. He began to cry as he prayed.

When I placed my hand on his shoulder, he looked up, the tears streaming down his face as he said, "I'm sorry! I'm sorry! I won't do it again! Please forgive me." Instantly I realized that he was apologizing for taking money from the offering plate. I stood speechless for a moment, bewildered by his unexpected confession.

It was our first spiritual breakthrough. I had not had to play detective, confront the culprit with his misdeed, or pressure him to confess. Here in a single night, during a season of prayer, Problem Number One (out of seemingly thousands) was solved.

That evening, when I was at my lowest, confounded by obstacles, bewildered by the darkness that surrounded us, unable even to continue preaching, I discovered an astonishing truth: God is attracted to weakness. He can't resist those who humbly and honestly admit how desperately they need him. Our weakness, in fact, makes room for his power.

I discovered an astonishing truth: God is attracted to weakness. He can't resist those who humbly and honestly admit how desperately they need him. ❦

In a parallel vein, people are not put off by honesty, either. I didn't have to keep up a ministerial front. I could just preach God's Word as best I knew and then call the congregation to prayer and worship. The Lord would take over from there.

How I treasure those early humblings. Those experiences showed me that I didn't need to play the preacher. Jesus called fishermen, not graduates of rabbinical schools. The main requirement was to be natural and sincere. His disciples had to depend totally upon the Lord and his power. In the same way, I had to stop trying to act ministerial—whatever that was. God could only use Jim Cymbala the way he is. What a breakthrough that was for me as I learned to trust in God to use my natural personality. God has always despised sham and pretense, especially in the pulpit. The minute I started trying to effect a posture or pose, God's Spirit would be grieved.

What I could do, however, was to get even more serious about studying. I began building a biblical library and giving many hours during the week to digging into God's Word. But another John Wesley or G. Campbell Morgan I would never be—that was obvious. I had to find my own style and stay open and dependent on God.

ON THE RAGGED EDGE

EVERY WEEK SEEMED TO carry with it a new challenge. The burner went out on the heating system and would cost $500 to repair. Unfortunately, my impassioned efforts as a fundraiser mustered only $150 in pledges from the people. I thought more than ever about quitting. *I'm not cut out for this,* I told myself. *I don't have that ministerial flair. I don't have a pastoral voice. I'm not an orator. I look too young. I'm so tired. . . .*

Neither Carol nor I knew where to turn for support. My parents lived in another part of Brooklyn, but my father was battling alcoholism at that point, and my mother was consumed with the struggle. So we couldn't rely much on her for encouragement.

The mother of one of Carol's friends heard what we were doing and dropped by one Sunday. She didn't say it, but you could tell what she was thinking: *What's a nice young couple like you doing down here?* It didn't take long to discover that most middle-class white Christians in other parts of the city did not find our location or congregation very attractive.

Some of the members we inherited were so out of step with the flavor of the church, so set on their own agenda, that I actually began to pray they would leave. One man informed me that he, too, was ordained and should be allowed to preach on Sunday nights. What I observed in his spiritual life, however, indicated just the opposite.

Confrontation came hard because we could ill afford to lose people. But if these members were to stay, the result would be ongoing discord—and I knew the Lord would never bless that kind of a mess with the spiritual power we so desperately needed. One by one, these people made their exit. On a couple of occasions I even had to help answer my own prayers by suggesting that members consider another church. I was learning that in pastoral work, as in basketball, sometimes you have to confront.

In time, despite these defections, the congregation was no longer twenty; it grew to forty or forty-five. The finances remained touch-and-go. Friends sometimes left bags of groceries on our doorstep, for which we were grateful. My first year in Brooklyn we received a total of $3,800 in salary. (The national average income for a household our size was $14,000!) The second year we climbed all the way to $5,200.

On more than one wintry Saturday night, I would think about the fact that attendance the next morning would probably be low because of the snow—most of our people couldn't afford cars. This would mean an even smaller offering. At such times I wondered how I could possibly face another Sunday. I even hoped that by some miracle the sun wouldn't come up the next morning.

Carol started a little choir with a grand total of nine voices. But problems soon arose there, too. No sooner did the choir begin to sing in the meetings than one of the girls in it got pregnant out of wedlock. In a small congregation everyone notices everything; everyone *talks about* everything.

After we had some Sunday night times of prayer around the altar, when people got into the habit of calling on the Lord, our attendance grew to fifty or sixty. But I knew God wanted to do much more . . . and he would, if we provided good soil in which he could work. I was tired of the escapist mentality I had witnessed since childhood—always glorifying what God did way back in some revival, or else passionately predicting "the coming great move of God" just ahead. The truth is, I knew there were countless churches across the city and the nation that had not baptized a hundred truly converted sinners in a year, and most not in several years. Any growth came simply through transfers from one church to another. New York City was a hard mission field, but transfer growth was not what God had in mind for us.

What we needed instead was a fresh wind and fresh fire. We needed the Holy Spirit to transform the desperate lives of people all around us. Alcohol and heroin dominated the neighborhood; LSD was also a problem, and cocaine was starting its wicked rise. Prostitutes were working a couple of street corners within three blocks of the church. Urban decay had clearly set in. Anybody who could make any money was trying to get *away* from our area.

I despaired at the thought that my life might slip by without seeing God show himself mightily on our behalf. Carol and I didn't want merely to mark time. I longed and cried out for God to change everything—me, the church, our passion for people, our praying.

> **I despaired at the thought that my life might slip by without seeing God show himself mightily on our behalf.** ❧

One day I told the Lord that I would rather die than merely tread water throughout my career in the ministry ... always preaching about the power of the Word and the Spirit, but never seeing it. I abhorred the thought of just having more church services. I hungered for God to break through in our lives and ministry.

THE PROMISE

ABOUT THAT TIME, I came down with a cough that would not go away. I hacked and hacked for six weeks, to the point that Carol could hardly get any sleep at night. I was spitting up phlegm every day.

My in-laws became so concerned that they paid my airfare to come down to their home near St. Petersburg, Florida, and get some rest in the warm sunshine. Gratefully, I headed their way. The only bad part was leaving Carol and two-year-old Chrissy behind.

One day I went out on a party fishing boat with twenty or thirty tourists. The sky was an azure blue, and the warm waters of the Gulf of Mexico lapped soothingly against the sandy shore. Seagulls swooped and squawked overhead. The sun felt good for my congested lungs.

As we launched out toward deep water, the others laughed and talked about the fish they hoped to catch that afternoon. I held a pole in my hands, too . . . but my mind wasn't on fishing. I moved down toward the end of the boat, away from the crowd, and stared at the far horizon.

I began mulling over the many ideas and strategies I had heard or read on church growth. One Christian leader had told me, "Forget about the institutional church *building*; home meetings are where it's at these days. You might as well sell your building; God is doing a new thing."

A once-large and historic Baptist church a few blocks away had invested heavily in a fleet of buses, trying to bring in large numbers of children. The only results were high insurance rates, chronic vandalism, and an unchanged church.

I had attended larger churches that seemed to center on bringing in popular speakers and singers, whoever was hot at the moment. This helped market the church . . . at least to other Christians. As one pastor told me with a smile, "I don't 'steal sheep' from other churches, but I do like to leave my gate wide open."

> **The embarrassing truth is that sometimes even *I* didn't want to show up for a service—that's how bad it was.** 🍃

Whether that was a valid approach or not, it took money, so forget it—nobody would come to downtown Brooklyn for the little honorarium we could afford. Moreover, Carol and I had frankly admitted to each other that unless God broke through, the Brooklyn Tabernacle was doomed. We couldn't finesse it along. We couldn't organize and market and program our way out. The embarrassing truth was that sometimes even *I* didn't want to show up for a service—that's how bad it was.

We *had* to have a visitation of the Holy Spirit, or bust.

"Lord, I have no idea how to be a successful pastor," I prayed softly out there on the water. "I haven't been trained. All I know is that Carol and I are working in the middle of New York City, with people dying on every side, overdosing from heroin, consumed by materialism, and all the rest. If the gospel is so powerful . . ."

I couldn't finish the sentence. Tears choked me. Fortunately, the others on the boat were too far away to notice as they studied their lines in the blue-green water.

Then quietly but forcefully, in words heard not with my ear but deep within my spirit, I sensed God speaking:

If you and your wife will lead my people to pray and call upon my name, you will never lack for something fresh to preach. I will supply all the money that's needed, both for the church and for your family, and you will never have a building large enough to contain the crowds I will send in response.

I was overwhelmed. My tears intensified. I looked up at the other passengers, still occupied with their fishing. Nobody glanced in my direction.

I knew I had heard from God, even though I had not experienced some strange vision, nothing sensational or peculiar. God was simply focusing on the only answer to our situation—or anybody else's, for that matter. His word to me was grounded in countless promises repeated in the Scriptures; it was the very thing that had produced every revival of the Holy Spirit throughout history. It was the truth that had made Charles G. Finney, Dwight L. Moody, A. B. Simpson, and other men and women mightily used of God. It was what I already knew, but God was now drawing me out, pulling me toward an actual experience of himself and his power. He was telling me that my hunger for him and his transforming power would be satisfied as I led my tiny congregation to call out to him in prayer.

As the boat docked later that afternoon, I felt wonderfully calm. A few days later I flew back to New York, still the same young pastor I had always been. But all the modern trends and new ideas about church growth were now irrelevant. God had promised to provide, to respond to our cries for divine help. We were not alone, attempting the impossible in a heartless world. God was present, and he would act on our behalf.

A holy excitement came over me. I actually looked forward to the next Sunday morning on Atlantic Avenue.

TWO

Catching Fire

WELCOME BACK, PASTOR CYMBALA," people said when they saw me that morning. "Did you have a good rest in Florida? How's your cough?"

I told them my cough was much better, but inside, I couldn't wait to tell them something far more important. Early in the service I said, "Brothers and sisters, I really feel that I've heard from God about the future of our church. While I was away, I was calling out to God to help us—to help *me*—understand what he wants most from us. And I believe I've heard an answer.

"It's not fancy or profound or spectacular. But I want to say to you today with all the seriousness I can muster: *From this day on, the prayer meeting will be the barometer of our church. What happens on Tuesday night will be the gauge by which we will judge success or failure because that will be the measure by which God blesses us.*

"If we call upon the Lord, he has promised in his Word to answer, to bring the unsaved to himself, to pour out his Spirit among us. If we don't call upon the Lord, he has promised nothing—nothing at all. It's as simple as that. No matter what I preach or what we claim to believe in our heads, the future will depend upon our times of prayer.

"This is the engine that will drive the church. Yes, I want you to keep coming on Sundays—but Tuesday night is what it's really all about. Carol and I have set our course, and we hope you'll come along with us."

A minister from Australia (or perhaps it was New Zealand) happened to be present that morning—a rare occurrence. I introduced him and invited him to say a few words. He walked to the front and made just one comment:

"I heard what your pastor said. Here's something to think about:

"You can tell how popular a church is by who comes on Sunday morning.

"You can tell how popular the pastor or evangelist is by who comes on Sunday night.

"But you can tell how popular Jesus is by who comes to the prayer meeting."

And with that, he walked off the platform. That was all. I never saw him again.

The New Beginning

If my announcement to that congregation sounds strange and overbearing, consider that it was not a whole lot different from what Charles Haddon Spurgeon, the great British pulpiteer, had said in a sermon almost exactly a hundred years before:

> The condition of the church may be very accurately gauged by its prayer meetings. So is the prayer meeting a grace-ometer, and from it we may judge of the amount of divine working among a people. If God be near a church, it must pray. And if he be not there, one of the first tokens of his absence will be a slothfulness in prayer.[1]

That first Tuesday night, fifteen to eighteen people showed up. I had no agenda or program laid out; I just stood up and led the people in singing and praising God. Out of that came extended prayer. I felt a new sense of unity and love among us. God seemed to be knitting us together. I didn't preach a typical sermon; there was new liberty to wait on God's presence.

In the weeks that followed, answers to prayer became noticeable. New people gradually joined, with talents and skills that could help us. Unsaved relatives and total strangers began to show up. We started to think of ourselves as a "Holy Ghost emergency room" where people in spiritual trauma could be rescued. In most hospitals, the ER isn't decorated as beautifully or fashionably as the rest of the building, but it's very efficient in saving lives.

> **We began to think of ourselves as a "Holy Ghost emergency room" where people in spiritual trauma could be rescued.**

We were a prime example of what the great Scottish devotional writer Andrew Bonar wrote in 1853: "God likes to see His people shut up to this, that there is no hope but in prayer. Herein lies the Church's power against the world."[2]

So week after week, I kept encouraging the people to pray. And of course, as Samuel Chadwick said long ago, the greatest answer to prayer is more prayer.

We were not there to hear one another give voice to eloquent prayers; we were too desperate for that. We focused vertically, on God, rather than horizontally on one another. Much of the time we called out to the Lord as a group, all praying aloud in concert, a practice that continues to this day. At other times we would join hands in circles of prayer, or various people would speak up with a special burden to express.

The format of a prayer meeting is not nearly as important as its essence—touching the Almighty, crying out with one's whole being. I have been in noisy prayer meetings that were mainly a show. I have been with groups in times of silent prayer that were deeply spiritual. The atmosphere of the meeting may vary; what matters most is that we encounter the God of the universe, not just each other.

I also began to ease up in the Sunday meetings and not control them so tightly with a microphone. The usual format—two songs, then announcements, special music by the choir, the offering, then the sermon, finally a benediction—was gradually laid aside as God began to loosen me up. I didn't have to be so nervous or uptight—or phony. I had only been protecting myself out of fear.

After all, people weren't hungry for fancy sermons or organizational polish. They just wanted love. They wanted to know that God could pick them up and give them a second chance.

People weren't hungry for fancy sermons or organizational polish. They just wanted love. ❧

In those early days on Atlantic Avenue, as people drew near to the Lord, received the Spirit's fullness, and rekindled their first love for God, they naturally began to talk about it on their jobs, in their apartment buildings, at family gatherings. Soon they were bringing new people.

From that day to the present, more than two decades later, there has never been a season of decline in the church, thank God. By his grace we have never had a faction rise up and decide to split away. God has continued to send people who need help; often I can't even find out how they learned of us.

The offerings improved to the point that we could make some building repairs. We replaced the tumbledown pews with fiberglass chairs that locked together. More important, however, people began to sense the presence of the Lord in that humble place. They felt loved. Hardened people would come in and break down even during the singing. The choir began to grow.

SOUNDS OF REJOICING

CAROL HAD LOVED MUSIC from the time she was a teenager. She came by it honestly—her father had been an opera singer before his conversion, and her grandmother was a pianist.

Growing up around the city meant that she had absorbed the sounds of many cultures. Inside her head, the classics blended with black gospel, traditional Scandinavian hymns with contemporary worship choruses and Caribbean rhythms. At the age of only sixteen or seventeen, a dream had entered her heart of directing a large choir someday—not a stiff, formal choir, but a choir of the common people.

Carol did not have a competent accompanist at the church, so she had to play the piano and lead the group simultaneously. She doesn't know how to read music, so she figured out the songs in her head and then taught the group by rote. Even so, the number of singers began to climb, eventually reaching fifty or so. The platform was not nearly large enough to hold them; they would just stand all across the front and sing, overwhelming the small building with their sound.

Practices were held on Friday nights. That may surprise readers who find that other weekend events would be too stiff a competition for people's time. But the urban schedule is different; people are too rushed during the week with their jobs and the long commutes on trains, buses, and subways. They finally relax when Friday evening comes, knowing they don't have to get up early the next day.

Carol would begin with a half hour of prayer. Often a spirit of worship fell on the group. Someone might volunteer a testimony or feel impressed to read Scripture. Carol might offer a short exhortation. Many nights there was more prayer and worship than there was practicing; sometimes the choir never got around to singing at all.

This experience put people in a whole different frame of mind. The choir wasn't just coming up with two "specials" to sing before the sermon; rather, the members were engaged in full-scale ministry.

The band members were as untrained as Carol. Joey Vazquez, who became the bass player, learned the instrument "on the job." He had been plunking around on a bass at a friend's house one day; at choir practice the next night, his friend jokingly said that Joey knew how to play. Carol assumed the friend was serious and put Joey to work. That was the beginning of his career as a bass player; he is still with the church today.

Our drummer, Michael Archibald, a man from Trinidad, has likewise never had lessons. Jonathan Woodby, our organist (and one of the best in America, we think), cannot read music. Yet these two have performed on two Grammy Award-winning albums.

The choir played a crucial role when we started hosting monthly rallies in cooperation with Teen Challenge, a ministry to drug addicts and gang members that was started in Brooklyn in 1958 by David Wilkerson. Together with Teen Challenge, we rented a big Baptist church. For the first rally we advertised the film *The Cross and the Switchblade*, which tells the conversion story of the notorious gang leader Nicky Cruz.

The crowd was so large we had to show the film three times that night so that everyone would get a chance to see it.

For the next rally, Nicky himself came to speak. It was amazing; here he was, preaching in the very building where years before, out on the steps, he had knocked out some Italian guy, ready to kill him if the cops hadn't showed up.

Nicky's story was a great inspiration to me. He was a symbol of things to come in our church: God taking hopeless, even crazy people and changing them. I knew that a lot of churches gave lip service to the idea that God can do anything. But we needed to have real faith that anyone who walked in, regardless of his or her problems, could become a trophy of God's grace. Ever since that night, Nicky has been a close friend of mine and a frequent guest at the Tabernacle.

As more churches got involved in the rallies, Carol formed a multiracial "New York Challenge Choir" made up of people from the Tabernacle plus any others who wanted to sing—eighty or more voices altogether.

It was about this time also that Carol wrote her first song. She took the Christmas carol "Joy to the World" and created a new melody for it. Again, she didn't know how to write it down, but simply taught it to the choir by rote.

A COMMUNITY OF LOVE AND PRAYER

WE NEVER KNEW WHO might come to Christ at the Brooklyn Tabernacle. There were junkies, prostitutes, and homosexuals. But lost lawyers, business types, and bus drivers turned to the Lord there, too. We welcomed them all.

There were Latinos, African Americans, Caribbean Americans, whites—you name it. Once people were energized by the Holy Spirit, they began to see other races as God's creation. Instead of railing at homosexuals, we began to weep over them. People began driving thirty or forty minutes from Long Island. The one—and perhaps only—advantage of our location in downtown Brooklyn is that excellent mass transit was available, which meant that people from Manhattan, Queens, the Bronx, and elsewhere could reach us easily on the subways and buses. By the time we grew to 150 or 175 on Sunday morning, the prayer meeting was up to 100. There was life, joy, a sense of family, and love. When a meeting ended, people weren't in a hurry to leave; they lingered and prayed and talked to one another.

There was no air-conditioning, so on hot summer nights we would have all the windows open and people even sitting on the sills. One Sunday night in August, when it was 90 degrees outside and probably 100 degrees in the building, I felt oddly impressed to lead "Silent Night, Holy Night" as an expression of love to Jesus. A drunk was passing by and stopped to listen. In his confused brain, he said to himself, *This drinking problem of mine is getting totally out of hand. Now I'm hearing Christmas carols. I'd better go in this church and get some help!* The ushers were there to meet him and minister to him.

The mentally disturbed could drop by as well. A fellow named Austin, recently released from an institution, started coming to church. One Sunday he said something vulgar to one of our women. When I called him on Tuesday and warned him that this wouldn't be tolerated, he said, "Oh yeah? I'm going to come take care of you with my 'boys.'" He was a huge man, so I didn't laugh.

I replied, "Austin, you might take care of me, but not with your 'boys'—the way you act, I doubt you have any 'boys.'"

I alerted the ushers that if he showed up again, they should call me—and also immediately call the police. That very night, Austin came back. I left the prayer meeting and went out to talk with him, stalling for time. Soon the police burst through the door and took him away. They wanted me to press charges, but I declined. Instead, I went back in and rejoined the prayer meeting. Episodes as strange as this became a regular part of ministering in this section of the city.

> **Because I had been a basketball player, it never dawned on me to evaluate people on the basis of color. In America it would appear that there is more openness in the gym than in the church of Jesus Christ.** 🌿

The offerings, as one might expect, were never great because of the kind of community we served, characterized by single mothers, people on public assistance, people seeking to become free of drugs. But people who were settled and secure were coming, too, who didn't mind the socioeconomic mix.

Because I had been a basketball player, it never dawned on me to evaluate people on the basis of color. If you could play, you could play. In America it would appear that there is more openness, acceptance, and teamwork in the gym than in the church of Jesus Christ.

SPACE PROBLEMS

BY 1977 MORE PEOPLE were trying to fit into the pews on Sunday morning and Sunday night than there was room for. Down the block was a YWCA with an auditorium that could seat 400 to 500 people. We were able to rent it on Sundays and began lugging our sound equipment and other supplies down there every week. The windows were painted shut, and there was no air-conditioning. Often we had to sweep out the place on Sunday morning before we could set up chairs for church.

But at least we had space to use. We rented the YWCA for two years. Some of the earliest memories of church for our two younger children, Susan and James, are in that building. I remember glancing up during the singing one Sunday and seeing, to my horror, my acrobatic preschool daughter turning 360-degree flips on some parallel bars over on the edge of the hall. So much for the "perfect pastor's kids"!

When Lanny Wolfe, a well-known gospel singer and songwriter, visited a service, he was captivated by the choir's sound, now up to one hundred voices. He encouraged Carol to write more. "You have an eclectic feel that's totally different," he said. "The songs you write are unlike anything I would do, or Bill Gaither, or anyone else." Lanny's encouragement meant a great deal to both of us.

Since then, of course, Carol's music has gone far and wide across the country and is sung in all kinds of churches, whatever the style of their worship. After selling one million units of Brooklyn Tabernacle sheet music, Word Music gave Carol an award in 1994. Ironically, the Tabernacle has not bought a single piece of her music—it wouldn't do any good for a choir that doesn't read music.

Meeting in the YWCA was a temporary solution, at best, to the overcrowding. We purchased a lot across the street in the hope of erecting a real church building one day. It required a big step of faith, but God provided the funds.

We scheduled a groundbreaking ceremony, excited about starting a new building, a permanent home. Would you believe that on that special Sunday, it rained so hard we couldn't go outdoors to put a shovel in the ground? Disappointed, we packed ourselves back into the Y auditorium that evening.

But in that meeting God clearly spoke to us that it wasn't the ground across the street he wanted to break. Instead, he would break our hearts and build his church on that foundation.

The downpour, as it turned out, was providential. A few months later, a large 1,400-seat theater on Flatbush Avenue, the main north-south artery of Brooklyn, became available for only $150,000.

We were able to sell the lot at a profit. We needed to sell the run-down Atlantic Avenue building as well in order to buy the theater. Some pastors came to look at our old place and appeared serious about buying it. We agreed on a price—only to find out later they hadn't even tried to secure a mortgage. By then we were in danger of losing our option on the theater.

All our dreams were about to come crashing down. At a Tuesday night prayer meeting we laid the problem before God, weeping and pleading for a last-minute rescue of some kind.

On Wednesday afternoon the doorbell at the church rang. I went downstairs to answer. There stood a well-dressed stranger, who, it turned out, was a Kuwaiti businessman. He walked in and looked around while I held my breath lest he look too closely at crooked walls, dingy bathrooms, and questionable plumbing. The basement ceiling was so low I feared he would hit his head on one of the pipes that hung down.

"What are you asking for this building?" he said at last.

I cleared my throat and answered weakly, "Ninety-five thousand."

He paused a moment and then said, "That's fair."

I was shocked!

He continued, "We have a deal."

"Uh, well, how long will it take you to make arrangements at the bank?" I was still worried that our option on the Flatbush property would expire before we could close this deal.

"No bank, nothing," he answered abruptly. "Just get your lawyer to call my lawyer—here's the name and phone number. Cash deal." And with that, he was gone.

Once again, our prayer had been answered in a surprising way.

God had formed a core of people who wanted to pray, who believed that nothing was too big for him to handle. No matter what roadblock we faced, no matter what attack came against us, no matter how wild the city became in the late seventies—as cocaine arrived on top of heroin, and then crack cocaine on top of that—God could still change people and deliver them from evil. He was building his church in a tough neighborhood, and as long as people kept calling out for his blessing and help, he had fully committed himself to respond.

THREE

A Song for the Desperate

Aᴌᴛʜᴏᴜɢʜ ᴛʜᴇ ᴛʜᴇᴀᴛᴇʀ ᴏɴ Flatbush seemed a treasure to us, it was in wretched shape. We spent more than $250,000 fixing it up before we could move in, in January 1979. That was when things really began to take off spiritually.

We had been in the Flatbush building less than a year when someone with connections to a Manhattan recording studio came along and suggested that the choir do what is called a "custom album"—a low-budget production for our own use. We did that in 1980, with Carol composing three or four of the ten works.

Somehow copies made their way to Nashville, and music companies began to approach us. Word Music repackaged the first album and offered it for sale across the country. They soon asked us to do two more. The choir ended up recording with everyone from Larnelle Harris to Babbie Mason to Wayne Watson to the Talleys to West Coast praise and worship leader Morris Chapman.

On Sundays it was not unusual for the choir to sing and testify with such anointing that a spirit of praise would descend on the people, changing the whole direction of the meeting. Once the choir had planned to do three songs. To introduce the second one, a former drug addict gave his testimony. There was such a powerful sense of God's love that I couldn't help walking up as the song was ending, putting one

39

arm around the fellow, and making an invitation right then for people to receive Christ. The response was immediate and strong.

The choir never got around to singing the third song—but after all, why should we hang onto some order of service if people were willing to get saved? God could use the choir, or anyone else, to turn the whole service into a prayer meeting if he wished.

BACK FROM THE "DEAD"

AMONG THE MANY PEOPLE whom the Lord touched in those days—initially through the choir but also through the Tuesday night prayer meeting—one who stands out was a slender, red-haired young woman named Roberta Langella. Her story is so amazing, I will let her tell it:

I WAS BORN THE FOURTH of six children in Brooklyn and raised on Staten Island. My father was a longshoreman who provided a good living and a Catholic education for all of us. I was happy to be part of what I thought was a stable, loving home.

But then, when I was only eleven, the wheels came off. All of a sudden, we were moving to Florida to be near my mother's parents. The only trouble was, Dad wasn't coming with us. I had failed to recognize the tension that had developed between my parents and had ruptured their marriage.

I just couldn't believe what was happening. Our family had always stuck together. If you couldn't rely on grown-ups to do the right thing, what was life all about anyway? I was shattered.

Within a year or two, I was acting out my unhappiness by drinking and smoking pot. My mom remarried, which only made matters worse as far as I was concerned. We fought all the time. At age sixteen I came back to New York to live with my dad for a year. That wasn't much better; I dropped out of school and took off to crisscross the country on my own.

A year later, I was back in New York living with a man twice my age. I just wanted somebody—anybody—to love me and take care of me. Unfortunately, this guy was an IV drug abuser. Before long, we were both on cocaine and then heroin. I ended up overdosing several times.

One terrible night in 1980 I shot up so many drugs that people said my heart actually stopped beating. My boyfriend took off, afraid that I had died and that he'd be left to answer incriminating questions. I was abandoned on that rooftop, turning blue ... but by God's grace someone discovered me and called 911. The paramedics came and revived me.

I felt so bad about myself, I was sure nobody thought I was worth anything. That led to one destructive relationship after another. Around 1982 my then current boyfriend and I rented a second-floor apartment above a florist shop next door to the Brooklyn Tabernacle. Of course, we hadn't the slightest interest in what went on there.

My boyfriend was abusive; he punched me out regularly. One day he beat me so badly he broke my eardrum. But every time it happened I would plead, "Don't leave me." It was so pathetic! But worse than being beaten, worse than being hated, was the terrifying thought of being left alone. I couldn't stand it.

I remember one Sunday afternoon when I was so distraught I threatened him. "I'm going to take my life," I said. Sprawled out on the couch, watching a football game, he didn't look up. "I'm watching the Jets now. Talk to me at half-time." He didn't even care!

I somehow kept functioning, working as a bartender in nightclubs. I was totally into the punk culture of the eighties—featuring the "dead look," where I didn't brush my hair for a month.

I remember frequenting "shooting galleries," where twenty or thirty people were getting high all at once, sharing needles. Although I was afraid of the consequences of sharing those needles, I was even more desperate for the drugs.

After the Greenwich Village bars closed in the early hours of the morning, I would proceed to the after-hours scene, which is crazy even to the crazy people. You really don't want to know the outrageous and violent things that go on in the clubs, lasting even past sunup.

Finally I would head home. As I would walk up out of the subway in my black leather jacket, there would be a sidewalk full of church people—all waiting to get into the Tabernacle. I would grit my teeth as I walked past. All their happy faces made me so angry!

Pushing through the crowd, I'd dash upstairs as fast as I could. The only trouble was, my bedroom window faced the alley toward the church, and I couldn't escape the music coming through the walls ... songs like "How Jesus Loves" and "I'm Clean." I'd listen to the melodies and sometimes break down. Something in the music would touch me, even though I didn't want to be touched.

But go inside the church? No way. I was sure Jesus could never love someone as strung out as I was.

Before long, my boyfriend and I split up—as usual—and I moved on to another relationship, another apartment on the Upper West Side of Manhattan. Sometimes I'd hear the woman one floor below singing in the shower. I met her in the hall one day and said, "I hear you singing sometimes. Are you a musician?"

"No, not really. I just sing in a choir at my church, and I like to practice the songs at home."

"What church is that?" I asked.

"The Brooklyn Tabernacle."

I had moved away, but that church kept moving in on me.

Meanwhile, the drug and alcohol abuse intensified. At times we had no food in the house; the phone was turned off. We started selling furniture in order to finance my drug habit. Somehow, though, I always held onto a job. All-night highs wouldn't keep me from getting up in the morning and going to work.

One evening at a friend's house, I broke down crying. For the first time in my life, I said, "You know, I think I might have a drug problem." That was the understatement of the decade, but an important first step for me.

Over the next few days I zeroed in on what I felt had to be the cause of my problems: my boyfriend. His drug use was a bad influence on me, right? So I kicked him out.

Within a few weeks, I had a new live-in boyfriend who didn't do drugs. Instead, he was a *dealer!* He'd bring pounds of cocaine into the house. Obviously, I kept using.

One night I called my mother in Florida, who by then had become a Christian. I started talking about my life—and couldn't stop. I don't know how she managed it, but she replied calmly to my agonized self-revelations by inviting me to come down and spend a couple of days with her.

Those few days in Florida stretched out to fourteen months. My mom got me into Narcotics Anonymous, and I went clean. I also managed, after all the years, to get my GED—my General Equivalency Diploma. Things were finally looking up, and I was sure I could conquer the world. But my newfound confidence came crashing down all too soon.

A visit to the doctor unveiled a horrible fact: I was HIV-positive. After all the needle-sharing over the years, I shouldn't have been surprised. But I became furious at this news, coming just as I was trying hard to get my act together. I was mad at myself and at God.

I returned to New York and started my own business. In the meantime, my brother Stephen had found the Lord and began witnessing to me, but I brushed him off. Finally I agreed to go with him to the Brooklyn Tabernacle, insisting on sitting in the balcony, arriving late and leaving early.

> **"Finally I hit bottom, at the end of a five- or six-day crack binge. It was a Tuesday night when I ran out of money. For some reason I drove to the church."—ROBERTA LANGELLA** ❦

It was only a matter of time until the siren call of drugs broke through my resolve. I lapsed back into the world of crack cocaine after two years of living clean. Inside, the old feelings of embarrassment and shame rose up again. But I just couldn't help it. I wanted the rush of drugs more than I wanted to keep struggling with life alone.

Finally I hit bottom, at the end of a five- or six-day crack binge. It was a Tuesday night when I ran out of money. For some reason I drove to the church—I don't know why. That night I found myself at the altar shedding tears I couldn't stop. "Oh, God, I need you in my life. Help me, please!" It was the moment of final surrender for me. From that point on, I began to believe God loved me. And with this newfound faith came hope and a slowly growing confidence.

A year later, I was actually singing in the very same choir I had so resented! My life was on steady ground after so much turmoil. I knew—I really knew down deep—that God loved me and accepted me and I could relax in his love. I was free of the chains that had bound me for so many years.

WE DIDN'T DISCOVER THIS wonderful miracle of God's grace until Roberta quietly sent Carol a seven-page letter. It was Easter time, and we were in the thick of planning a concert. Carol sat down to read this letter one evening and within minutes was weeping. "Jim—you have to stop and read this," she insisted, handing me the first page and then the next and the next. Soon I was in tears along with her.

When we finished, we looked at each other and said, "This is amazing. She *has* to tell her story at the Easter concert." Roberta had never spoken in public before, but she gamely agreed to try.

The day came, and the building was jammed. She had invited all her family. Many of them, including her father in the third row, didn't know the half of what they were about to hear.

After four choir numbers, Roberta came out of the choir, nervously picked up a microphone, and began to speak. "Hi, my name is Roberta Langella . . . and I want to tell you what the risen Jesus means to me."

We had coached her to leave out a few of the most lurid details, but even so, her story was powerful. As she got to the toughest parts, she couldn't help stopping to say, "Daddy . . . I know this is hard for you to hear. But I have to say it, because it shows how Jesus can forgive the worst in a person's life." The emotion was so incredible it took your breath away. People were on the edge of their seats.

The choir then sang the final song, and I brought the meeting to a close. The first person to the altar was Roberta's father, sobbing profusely. Then came her uncle, her aunt, and the rest of the clan.

Today Roberta Langella heads up our ministry called "New Beginnings," a weekly outreach to drug abusers and the homeless. She now has a hundred workers involved, riding the subway every Sunday afternoon to the shelters and rehab centers to escort people to our church for a meal and the evening meeting. The love of the Lord just exudes from her life.

Roberta is a real trooper these days, even when she doesn't feel well. As she sits in the balcony on Sunday nights with all the homeless she has brought with her, there's nobody too dirty, too far gone for her to care about. She sees herself in them. She is a living example of the power of God to pick up the downtrodden, the self-loathing, the addicted, and redeem them for his glory.

Secret "Formula"

Providing space for people such as Roberta and the scores of homeless she brings our way has turned out to be a perennial problem for us. In 1985 the overall growth of the church forced us to add an afternoon service at 3:30, and in early 1996, a fourth service—each of them two to two-and-a-half hours long. We have always felt we had to give the Holy Spirit time to work; we couldn't rush people through some kind of assembly line. The worship times are now 9:00 A.M., 12:00 noon, 3:30 P.M., and 7:30 P.M.

This makes a grueling schedule, but we have no choice until we can get into a larger facility. I simply cannot abide turning people away at the door, which is what has had to happen often.

With people in the overflow room plus the lobby sitting on stackable chairs and watching TV monitors, we can accommodate at least 1,600 per meeting. This increase has occurred in spite of the fact that around 1985 we began to send groups of people out to start churches in other parts of the city: the Glendale section of Queens, the Lower East Side of Manhattan, the South Bronx, Coney Island, Harlem, and so forth. The present count stands at seven churches in the greater New York area, plus another ten elsewhere, from New Hampshire to San Francisco and even overseas.

> **Each service is two to two-and-a-half hours long. We have always felt we had to give the Holy Spirit time to work; we couldn't rush people through some kind of assembly line. 🌿**

The first groups were launched with the help of the choir through public concerts. Actually, that first concert was something of an accident. A minister in Manhattan called me one day to ask a favor. He had booked the famous Carnegie Hall, which seats 2,100, on a Wednesday night for a Christian concert—and the artist had canceled with only forty-five days to go. Was there any way our choir could fill in and somehow prevent the financial loss that would otherwise occur, since Carnegie Hall was not about to let him out of his contract?

We had never done anything like that, and we didn't know how to go about it. Should we sell tickets? We elected to sing with no admission charge, taking an offering instead. The hall management was not happy about this arrangement but reluctantly agreed.

We began passing the word throughout the city that the Brooklyn Tabernacle Choir would premiere some of its new songs at a free concert. On the appointed day we got the shock of our lives when people began lining up outside the hall before noon! The line stretched from the door on West 57th Street up to the corner, down a full block on Seventh Avenue, around another corner along West 56th—3,500 people in all.

The next thing I knew, the New York Police Department was there with crowd-control barricades and officers on horseback. I was so embarrassed about my mishandling of the whole situation that I went inside and hid in a basement room. A stern-faced sergeant came looking for me to ask, "What's going on here? Who caused all this?" I sheepishly admitted it was my fault.

The concert was a wonderful success. Near the end I gave a brief presentation of the gospel the choir had been singing about, then I closed with a public invitation. People readily came forward to accept Christ. We prayed with them right there and collected their names and addresses for follow-up.

A few weeks later I received a phone call from someone at Radio City Music Hall. "Why don't you book with us next time? We seat six thousand."

Carol and I were honored by the invitation, but there was, of course, the small matter of the charges: more than $70,000! We took a deep breath and decided to make the plunge, understandably selling tickets this time in order to cover the expense. We promoted the night as the premiere of a new album.

The tickets sold out in three days.

The next time we released a choir album, we did two nights. For the *Live . . . With Friends* album, we ventured for three nights—and sold out all three. Each choir member was committed to trying to sell fifty tickets to people at work who didn't attend church. When a member would say, "Hey, I'm singing at Radio City Music Hall next month—would you like to buy a ticket?" people usually reacted with amazement—and an affirmative response.

Church planting became an important motive for the events. We would give away free tickets in whatever section of the city we wanted to start a church. Then during the concert we would announce, "This coming Sunday, services will begin at such-and-such a place; please join us there."

The biggest distributor of Christian choral music in America got acquainted with us, liked the music, and sat down with Carol one day to ask: "So what's the formula here? What makes this work?"

She began talking about the choir prayer meeting. The visitor said to himself, *She didn't understand my question. I want to know what makes the music so inspirational.*

It was months before he realized that the life in the music comes from prayer. That's the formula.

Prayer cannot truly be taught by principles and seminars and symposiums. It has to be born out of a whole environment of felt need. If I say, "I *ought* to pray," I will soon run out of motivation and quit; the flesh is too strong. I have to be *driven* to pray.

> **Yes, the roughness of inner-city life has pressed us to pray. . . . But is the rest of the country coasting along in fine shape? I think not.** ❧

Yes, the roughness of inner-city life has pressed us to pray. When you have alcoholics trying to sleep on the back steps of your building, when your teenagers are getting assaulted and knifed on the way to youth meetings, when you bump into transvestites in the lobby after church, you can't escape your need for God. According to a recent Columbia University study, twenty-one cents of every dollar New Yorkers pay in city taxes is spent trying to cope with the effects of smoking, drinking, and drug abuse.

But is the rest of the country coasting along in fine shape? I think not. In the smallest village in the Farm Belt, there are still urgent needs. Every congregation has wayward kids, family members who aren't serving God. Do we really believe that God can bring them back to himself?

Too many Christians live in a state of denial: "Well, I hope my child will come around someday." Some parents have actually given up: "I guess nothing can be done. Bobby didn't turn out right—but we tried; we dedicated him to the Lord when he was a baby. Maybe someday . . ."

The more we pray, the more we sense our need to pray. And the more we sense a need to pray, the more we *want* to pray.

CHECK THE VITAL SIGNS

PRAYER IS THE SOURCE of the Christian life, a Christian's life-line. Otherwise, it's like having a baby in your arms and dressing her up so cute—but she's not breathing! Never mind the frilly clothes; *stabilize the child's vital signs*. It does no good to talk to someone in a comatose state. That's why the great emphasis on teaching in today's churches is producing such limited results. Teaching is good only where there's life to be channeled. If the listeners are in a spiritual coma, what we're telling them may be fine and orthodox, but unfortunately, spiritual life cannot be taught.

Pastors and churches have to get uncomfortable enough to say, "We are not New Testament Christians if we don't have a prayer life." This conviction makes us squirm a little, but how else will there be a breakthrough with God?

If we truly think about what Acts 2:42 says—"They devoted themselves to the apostles' teaching and to the fellowship, to the breaking of bread and to prayer"—we can see that prayer is almost a proof of a church's normalcy. Calling on the name of the Lord is the fourth great hallmark in the list. If my church or your church isn't praying, we shouldn't be boasting in our orthodoxy or our Sunday morning attendance figures.

In fact, Carol and I have told each other more than once that if the spirit of brokenness and calling on God ever slacks off in the Brooklyn Tabernacle, we'll know we're in trouble, even if we have 10,000 in attendance.

FOUR

❧

The Greatest Discovery
of All Time

DURING COUNTLESS TUESDAY NIGHT prayer meetings I find myself encircled by the sacred sounds of prayer and intercession filling the church, spilling into the vestibule, and overflowing from every heart present. As the meeting edges to a close, I overhear mothers petitioning for wayward children ... men asking God to please help them find employment ... others giving thanks for recent answers to prayer ... tearful voices here and there. I can't help but think, *This is as close to heaven as I will ever get in this life. I don't want to leave here. If I were invited to the White House to meet some dignitary, it would never bring the kind of peace and deep joy I sense here in the presence of people calling on the Lord.*

The sound isn't forced, as if the crowd had been worked up into a religious frenzy. Rather, it is the sound of people freely expressing their hearts' needs, desires, and praises.

What I'm hearing on those Tuesday nights is not unusual or peculiar to our church. Far from being a new invention, this kind of prayer has ancient roots. It goes back before Christ, before David, even before Moses organized a formal worship system with the tabernacle. The first mention occurs all the way back in Genesis 4:25–26:

> Adam lay with his wife again, and she gave birth to a
> son and named him Seth, saying, "God has granted me

another child in place of Abel, since Cain killed him."
Seth also had a son, and he named him Enosh.

At that time men began to call on the name of the LORD.

Think about that. Until then, people had known God mainly as the Creator. He had made the Garden of Eden and the rest of the world as far as their eyes could see.

Now came the beginning of the first *collective relationship* with the Almighty. Before a Bible was available, before the first preacher was ordained or the first choir formed, a godly strain of men and women distinguished themselves from their ungodly neighbors by *calling on the Lord.* Cain and his posterity had gone their own way, independent of God. By contrast, these people affirmed their dependence on God by calling out to him.

In fact, God's first people were not called "Jews" or "the children of Israel" or "Hebrews." In the *very* beginning their original name was "those who call on the name of the LORD."

On some unmarked day . . . at some unnoted hour . . . a God-placed instinct in human hearts came alive. People sensed that if you are in trouble and you call out to God, he will answer you! He will intervene in your situation.

I can imagine one woman saying to another, "Have you heard about the God who answers when you call on him? He's more than just the Creator; he cares and responds to our needs. He actually understands what we're feeling."

"What are you talking about? God does whatever he pleases; people can't influence him one way or the other."

"No, no, you're wrong. When you call out to him, he doesn't turn a deaf ear. He listens! He responds. He acts."

"LORD, HELP!"

DAVID JEREMIAH, MY LONGTIME FRIEND from Shadow Mountain Community Church near San Diego, has preached several times at the Brooklyn Tabernacle. Immediately after being diagnosed with cancer, he called to ask us to pray. Several months later he returned to visit us during an outreach meeting we held at Madison Square Garden arena. Later he preached at one of our Sunday services. The whole congregation was delighted to see this wonderful Christian brother for whom we had all interceded.

> **God is not aloof. He says continually through the centuries, "I'll help you, I really will. When you're ready to throw up your hands— throw them up to me."** 🐦

Moved by the love and thanksgiving his appearance produced, David later remarked about it from the pulpit:

"I called here as soon as I learned of my sickness because I knew of your emphasis on prayer. In fact, someone just greeted me in the lobby and remarked, 'Pastor Jeremiah, we really cried out to God on your behalf.' That is why I called you. I knew your praying wouldn't be just some mechanical exercise but a real calling out to God with passion for my need. And God brought me through the ordeal."

That is the literal meaning of the Hebrew word used countless times in the Old Testament when people *called* upon God. It means *to cry out, to implore aid.* This is the essence of true prayer that touches God.

Charles Spurgeon once remarked that "the best style of prayer is that which cannot be called anything else but a cry."[1]

Isn't that what God *invites* us to do all through the Bible? "Call to me and I will answer you and tell you great and unsearchable things you do not know" (Jer. 33:3). God is not aloof. He is not disconnected. He says continually through the centuries, "I'll help you, I really will. When you don't know where to turn, then turn to me. When you're ready to throw up your hands—throw them up to me. Put your voice behind them, too, and I'll come and help you."

After Moses came down from Mount Sinai, calling on God became an earmark of his people's successes. The patriarch spotlighted this most dramatically in his farewell address: "What other nation is so great as to have their gods near them the way the LORD our God is near us whenever we pray to him?" (Deut. 4:7). The other nations may have had better chariots, better weaponry, but that wouldn't matter in the end. They didn't have what Israel had: a God who would respond when they called upon him. And note that there was no promised help from God if Israel ceased calling out to him. Only defeat and humiliation would follow.

THE REAL FORCE

SATAN'S MAIN STRATEGY WITH God's people has always been to whisper, "Don't call, don't ask, don't depend on God to do great things. You'll get along fine if you just rely on your own cleverness and energy." The truth of the matter is that the devil is not terribly frightened of our human efforts and credentials. But he knows his kingdom will be damaged when we lift up our hearts to God.

Listen to David's confident assertion in Psalm 4:3. "Know that the LORD has set apart the godly for himself; the LORD *will hear when I call to him*." That was David's whole posture, his instinct, and especially his approach to warfare. *It doesn't matter what the Philistine armies have. If we call out to God, he will give us the victory. If we backslide and don't call, then we can be defeated by a tiny army.*

I can almost hear David saying, "You can chase me, you can persecute me, you can do anything you want—but when I call on God, you're in trouble! The Lord will hear when I call to him."

....

The devil is not terribly frightened of our human efforts and credentials. But he knows his kingdom will be damaged when we begin to lift up our hearts to God. ❧

....

Notice how God defines wicked people in Psalm 14:4. "Will evildoers never learn—those who devour my people as men eat bread *and who do not call on the LORD?*" That is the divine definition of the ungodly. They will do many things, but they will not humble themselves and recognize God's omnipotence by calling on his name with all their hearts.

One of the great devotional writers said, "The main thing God asks for is our attention."

Salvation itself is impossible until a person humbly calls upon the name of the Lord (Acts 2:21), for God has promised specifically to be rich in mercy to those who call on his name (Rom. 10:12–13).

"Call upon me in the day of trouble," God says in Psalm 50:15. "I will deliver you, and you will honor me." God desires praise from our lives . . . but the only way fresh praise and honor will come is as we keep coming to him in times of need and difficulty. Then he will intervene to show himself strong on our behalf, and we will know that he has done it.

Are not we all prone to be a little cocky and think we can handle things just fine? But let some trouble come, and how quickly we sense our inadequacy. Trouble is one of God's

great servants because it reminds us how much we continually
need the Lord. Otherwise, we tend to forget about entreating
him. For some reason we want to carry on by ourselves.

HOW REVIVAL STARTS

THE HISTORY OF PAST revivals portray this truth in full color.
Whether you study the Great Awakening, the Second Great
Awakening, the Welsh Revival, the 1906 outpouring on Azusa
Street in Los Angeles, or any other period of revival, you
always find men and women who first inwardly groan, longing to see the status quo changed—in themselves and in their
churches. They begin to call on God with insistence; prayer
begets revival, which begets more prayer. It's like Psalm 80,
where Asaph bemoans the sad state of his time, the broken
walls, the rampaging animals, the burnt vineyards. Then in
verse 18 he pleads, "Revive us, and we will call on your name."

The Holy Spirit is the Spirit of prayer. Only when we are
full of the Spirit do we feel the need for God everywhere we
turn. We can be driving a car, and spontaneously our spirit
starts going up to God with needs and petitions and inter-
cessions right there in the middle of traffic.

If our churches don't pray, and if people don't have an
appetite for God, what does it matter how many are attending the services? How would that impress God? Can you
imagine the angels saying, "Oh, your pews! We can't believe
how beautiful they are! Up here in heaven, we've been talking about them for years. Your sanctuary lighting—it's so
clever. The way you have the steps coming up to the pulpit—
it's wonderful. . . ."

I don't think so.

If we don't want to experience God's closeness here on
earth, why would we want to go to heaven anyway? He is the

center of everything there. If we don't enjoy being in his presence here and now, then heaven would not be heaven for us. Why would he send anyone there who doesn't long for him passionately here on earth?

I am not suggesting that we are justified by works of prayer or any other acts of devotion. I am not a legalist. But let us not dodge the issue of what heaven will be like: enjoying the presence of God, taking time to love him, listening to him, and giving him praise.

I have talked with pastor after pastor, some of them prominent and "successful," who have told me privately, "Jim, the truth is, I couldn't have a real prayer meeting in my church. I'd be embarrassed at the smallness of the crowd. Unless somebody's teaching or singing or doing some kind of presentation, people just won't come. I can only get them for a one-hour service, and that only once a week."

Is that kind of religion found anywhere in the Bible? Jesus himself can't draw a crowd even among his own people! What a tragedy that the quality of ministry is too often measured by numbers and building size rather than by true spiritual results.

As a preacher myself, let me be blunt here. Preaching itself can easily become just a subtle form of entertainment. When I stand at the Judgment Seat of Christ, he is not going to ask me if I was a clever orator. He is not going to ask me how many books I wrote. He is only going to ask whether I continued in the line of men and women, starting way back in the time of Adam's grandchildren, who led others to call upon God.

A PERSONAL TEST

ALL MY TALKING ABOUT prayer faced a severe test several years ago when Carol and I went through the darkest two-and-a-half-year tunnel we could imagine.

Our oldest daughter, Chrissy, had been a model child growing up. But around age sixteen she started to stray. I admit I was slow to notice this—I was too occupied with the church, starting branch congregations, overseeing projects, and all the rest that ministry entails.

Meanwhile, Chrissy not only drew away from us, but also away from God. In time, she even left our home. There were many nights when we had no idea where she was.

As the situation grew more serious, I tried everything. I begged, I pleaded, I scolded, I argued, I tried to control her with money. Looking back, I recognize the foolishness of my actions. Nothing worked; she just hardened more and more. Her boyfriend was everything we did not want for our child.

How I kept functioning through that period I don't know. Many a Sunday morning I would put on my suit, get into the car to drive to the Tabernacle early, ahead of Carol . . . and cry for the next 25 minutes, all the way to the church door. "God, how am I going to get through three meetings today? I don't want to make myself the center of attention. The people have problems of their own—they're coming for help and encouragement. But what about me? I'm hanging by a thread. Oh, God, please . . . my firstborn, my Chrissy."

Somehow God would pull my nerves together enough for me to function through another long Sunday. There were moments, however, as we were worshiping God and singing, that my spirit would almost seem to run away from the meeting to intercede for Chrissy. I had to control myself to stay focused on the people and their needs.

While this was going on, we learned that Carol needed an operation—a hysterectomy. As she tried to adjust afterward, the devil took the opportunity to come after her and say, *You might have this big choir, and you're making albums and doing outreaches at Radio City Music Hall and all the rest. Fine,*

*you and your husband can go ahead to reach the world for Christ—
but I'm going to have your children. I've already got the first one.
I'm coming for the next two.*

Like any mother who loves her children, Carol was smitten with tremendous fear and distress. Her family meant more to her than a choir. One day she said to me, "Listen, we need to leave New York. I'm serious. This atmosphere has already swallowed up our daughter. We can't keep raising kids here. If you want to stay, you can—but I'm getting our other children out." She wasn't kidding.

> **One day Carol said to me, "Listen, we need
> to leave New York. I'm serious. We can't
> keep raising our kids in this atmosphere."** ❧

I said, "Carol, we just can't do that. We can't unilaterally take off without knowing what God wants us to do."

Carol wasn't being rebellious; she was just depressed after the surgery. She elected not to pack up and run after all. And it was at that low point that she went to the piano one day, and God gave her a song that has touched more people than perhaps anything else she has written:

In my moments of fear,
Through every pain, every tear,
There's a God who's been faithful to me.
When my strength was all gone,
When my heart had no song,
Still in love he's proved faithful to me.
Every word he's promised is true;
What I thought was impossible, I see my God do.

He's been faithful, faithful to me,
Looking back, his love and mercy I see.
Though in my heart I have questioned,
Even failed to believe,
Yet he's been faithful, faithful to me.

When my heart looked away,
The many times I could not pray,
Still my God, he was faithful to me.
The days I spent so selfishly,
Reaching out for what pleased me;
Even then God was faithful to me
Every time I come back to him,
He is waiting with open arms,
And I see once again.

He's been faithful, faithful to me. . . .[2]

Were we calling on the Lord through all of this? In a sense we were. But I couldn't help jumping in to take action on my own, too. I was still, to some degree, the point guard wanting to grab the basketball, push it down the floor, make something happen, press through any hole in the defense I could find. But the more I pressed, the worse Chrissy got.

Then one November, I was alone in Florida when I received a call from a minister whom I had persuaded Chrissy to talk to. "Jim," he said, "I love you and your wife, but the truth of the matter is, Chrissy's going to do what Chrissy's going to do. You don't really have much choice, now that she's eighteen. She's determined. You're going to have to accept whatever she decides."

I hung up the phone. Something very deep within me began to cry out. "Never! I will never accept Chrissy being away from you, Lord!" I knew that if she continued on the present path, there would be nothing but destruction awaiting her.

Once again, as back in 1972, there came a divine show-down. God strongly impressed me to stop crying, screaming, or talking to anyone else about Chrissy. I was to converse with no one but God. In fact, I knew I should have no further contact with Chrissy—until God acted! I was just to believe and obey what I had preached so often—

Call upon me in the day of trouble, and I will answer you.

I dissolved in a flood of tears. I knew I had to let go of this situation.

Back home in New York, I began to pray with an intensity and growing faith as never before. Whatever bad news I would receive about Chrissy, I kept interceding and actually began praising God for what I knew he would do soon. I made no attempts to see her. Carol and I endured the Christmas season with real sadness. I was pathetic, sitting around trying to open presents with our other two children, without Chrissy.

February came. One cold Tuesday night during the prayer meeting, I talked from Acts 4 about the church boldly calling on God in the face of persecution. We entered into a time of prayer, everyone reaching out to the Lord simultaneously.

An usher handed me a note. A young woman whom I felt to be spiritually sensitive had written: *Pastor Cymbala, I feel impressed that we should stop the meeting and all pray for your daughter.*

I hesitated. Was it right to change the flow of the service and focus on my personal need?

Yet something in the note seemed to ring true. In a few minutes I picked up a microphone and told the congregation what had just happened. "The truth of the matter," I said, "although I haven't talked much about it, is that my daughter is very far from God these days. She thinks up is down, and down is up; dark is light, and light is dark. But I know God can break through to her, and so I'm going to ask Pastor

Boekstaaf to lead us in praying for Chrissy. Let's all join hands across the sanctuary."

As my associate began to lead the people, I stood behind him with my hand on his back. My tear ducts had run dry, but I prayed as best I knew.

To describe what happened in the next minutes, I can only employ a metaphor: *The church turned into a labor room.* The sounds of women giving birth are not pleasant, but the results are wonderful. Paul knew this when he wrote, "My dear children, for whom I am again in the pains of childbirth until Christ is formed in you ..." (Gal. 4:19).

There arose a groaning, a sense of desperate determination, as if to say, "Satan, you will *not* have this girl. Take your hands off her—she's coming back!" I was overwhelmed. The force of that vast throng calling on God almost literally knocked me over.

When I got home that night, Carol was waiting up for me. We sat at the kitchen table drinking coffee, and I said, "It's over."

"What's over?" she wondered.

"It's over with Chrissy. You would have had to be in the prayer meeting tonight. I tell you, if there's a God in heaven, this whole nightmare is finally over." I described what had taken place.

BACK FROM THE ABYSS

THIRTY-TWO HOURS LATER, ON Thursday morning, as I was shaving, Carol suddenly burst through the door, her eyes wide. "Go downstairs!" she blurted. "Chrissy's here."

"Chrissy's *here?*"

"Yes! Go down!"

"But Carol—I—"

"Just go down," she urged. "It's you she wants to see."

I wiped off the shaving foam and headed down the stairs, my heart pounding. As I came around the corner, I saw my daughter on the kitchen *floor*, rocking on her hands and knees, sobbing. Cautiously I spoke her name:

"Chrissy?"

She grabbed my pant leg and began pouring out her anguish. "Daddy—Daddy—I've sinned against God. I've sinned against myself. I've sinned against you and Mommy. Please forgive me—"

My vision was as clouded by tears as hers. I pulled her up from the floor and held her close as we cried together.

Suddenly she drew back. "Daddy," she said with a start, *"who was praying for me? Who was praying for me?"* Her voice was like that of a cross-examining attorney.

"What do you mean, Chrissy?"

"On Tuesday night, Daddy—who was praying for me?"
I didn't say anything, so she continued:

"In the middle of the night, God woke me and showed me I was heading toward this abyss. There was no bottom to it—it scared me to death. I was so frightened. I realized how hard I've been, how wrong, how rebellious.

"But at the same time, it was like God wrapped his arms around me and held me tight. He kept me from sliding any farther as he said, 'I still love you.'

"Daddy, tell me the truth—*who was praying for me Tuesday night?*"

I looked into her bloodshot eyes, and once again I recognized the daughter we had raised.

Chrissy's return to the Lord became evident immediately. By that fall, God had opened a miraculous door for her to enroll at a Bible college, where she not only undertook studies but soon began directing music groups and a large choir, just like her mother. Today she is a pastor's wife in the Midwest with three wonderful children. Through all this, Carol and I learned as never before that persistent calling upon the Lord breaks through every stronghold of the devil, for nothing is impossible with God.

For Christians in these troubled times, there is simply no other way.

FIVE

❦

The Day Jesus Got Mad

LIKE MOST CHRISTIANS, I love the mental picture of Jesus the Good Shepherd putting the lamb on his shoulders and carrying it to safety.

I love the soft image of the Baby in the manger.

I love the story about Christ feeding the hungry multitudes with bread and fish.

When I think about Jesus dying on the cross to pay for my sin, I'm deeply moved.

I marvel at the sight of him bursting out of the tomb, alive on Resurrection morning.

But there is one picture of Jesus that, frankly, doesn't seem to fit. It is so stunning I wonder why God would even put it in the Bible ... not once, but twice. The second account is in Mark 11:15–18.

> On reaching Jerusalem, Jesus entered the temple area and began driving out those who were buying and selling there. He overturned the tables of the money changers and the benches of those selling doves, and would not allow anyone to carry merchandise through the temple courts. And as he taught them, he said, "Is it not written:
>
> "'My house will be called a house of prayer for all nations'?

But you have made it 'a den of robbers.'"

The chief priests and the teachers of the law heard this and began looking for a way to kill him, for they feared him, because the whole crowd was amazed at his teaching.

The twelve disciples were no doubt just as stunned as the crowd; nothing is said about their helping their Master clean house. All by himself Jesus started pitching over the tables, blocking people who were carrying things, and saying, "Get out of here with that! You can't bring that through the courts." He stormed over to the merchants of oxen and sheep and doves, saying, "Out! Get your business out of here!"

What happened to the loving Jesus? Anyone who gets that irate and physical surely must not be walking in the Spirit, right? But this was Jesus Christ. In fact, the first time he did this a couple of years before (see John 2), he even made a whip out of cords. He was physically thrashing people out of the temple!

What made God's Son so agitated?

His house was being prostituted *for purposes other than what was intended.*

As the feathers were flying and the coins were clattering to the pavement and the businessmen were shouting for the police, Jesus said above the roar, "This place looks and feels more like a mall than a temple. Whatever happened to Isaiah's word about the real point of this building—to be a house of prayer for all nationalities and races? Out! Get out, all of you!"

Just Doing Their Job

THE ODD THING ABOUT this event is that if Eyewitness News had interviewed any of the merchants that day, each would have vigorously defended the right to be there. "We provide an essential service to the worshipers," they would have said. "How else are people going to get the required animal to sacrifice? If you live any distance away, you can't be herding your sheep and cows through the streets of Jerusalem. We've got to help the program along. . . ." But, of course, they had added a gouging surcharge to the price.

> **Jesus is not terribly impressed with religious commercialism. He is concerned not only** *whether* **we're doing God's work, but also** *how and why* **we're doing it.** ❧

The money changers would have said the same. "Everybody has to pay the temple tax, and people can't be walking in here with Greek or Roman or Macedonian money. They've got to use the special coins minted here in Jerusalem. We help people with their currency problems." But once again, they were tacking on big-time profits.

For all of us involved in preaching the gospel, performing music, publishing Christian materials, and all the rest, there is an uncomfortable message here: Jesus is not terribly impressed with religious commercialism. He is concerned not only *whether* we're doing God's work, but also *how and why* we're doing it. At the Judgment Seat of Christ, his main questions for me will have to do not with the growth or the budget of the Brooklyn Tabernacle, but with *why* I pastored this church—in what spirit.

If you sing in a choir, the question is not just *if* you're on your note; it's *why* you are singing at all.

If you teach a class, are you doing it with a heart that radiates God's love for the students, or for some other reason?

I am dismayed at the contracts required by some contemporary Christian musical groups. To perform a concert at your church, the stated fee will be so much (in either four or five figures) plus round-trip airfare—often in first class, not coach. Every detail of the accommodations is spelled out, down to "sushi for twenty persons" waiting at the hotel, in one case. All this is done so that the group can stand before an inner-city audience and exhort the people to "just trust the Lord for all your needs."

Our forebears back in the camp meeting days used to say that if people left a meeting talking about what a wonderful sermon the preacher gave or how beautifully the singers sang, the meeting had failed. But if people went home saying things like "Isn't God good? He met me tonight in such a wonderful way," it was a good meeting. There was to be no sharing the stage with the Lord.

The first-century money changers were in the temple, but they didn't have the spirit of the temple. They may have played a legitimate role in assisting people to worship, but they were out of sync with the whole purpose of the Lord's house.

> **Does the Bible ever say anywhere from Genesis to Revelation, "My house shall be called a house of preaching"?** ❧

"The atmosphere of my Father's house," Jesus seemed to say, "is to be prayer. The aroma around my Father must be that of people opening their hearts in worship and supplication. This is not just a place to make a buck. This is a house for calling on the Lord."

I do not mean to imply that the Jerusalem temple, built by Herod the Great, is the direct counterpart of our church buildings today. God no longer centers his presence in one particular building. In fact, the New Testament teaches that *we* are now his dwelling place; he lives in his people. How much more important, then, is Jesus' message about the primacy of prayer?

> **I have seen God do more in people's lives during ten minutes of real prayer than in ten of my sermons.** ❧

The feature that is supposed to distinguish Christian churches, Christian people, and Christian gatherings is the aroma of prayer. It doesn't matter what your tradition or my tradition is. The house is not ours anyway; it is the Father's.

Does the Bible ever say anywhere from Genesis to Revelation, "My house shall be called a house of preaching"?

Does it ever say, "My house shall be called a house of music"?

Of course not.

The Bible does say, "My house shall be called a house of prayer for all nations." Preaching, music, the reading of the Word—these things are fine; I believe in and practice all of them. But they must never override prayer as the defining mark of God's dwelling. The honest truth is that I have seen God do more in people's lives during ten minutes of real prayer than in ten of my sermons.

THE CHURCH'S MAIN POINT

HAVE YOU EVER NOTICED that Jesus launched the Christian church, not while someone was preaching, but while people were praying? In the first two chapters of Acts, the disciples were doing nothing but waiting on God. As they were just sitting there ... worshiping, communing with God, letting God shape them and cleanse their spirits and do those heart operations that only the Holy Spirit can do ... the church was born. The Holy Spirit was poured out.

What does it say about our churches today that God birthed the church in a prayer meeting, and prayer meetings today are almost extinct?

> **What does it say about our churches today that God birthed the church in a prayer meeting, and prayer meetings today are almost extinct?** &

Am I the only one who gets embarrassed when religious leaders in America talk about having prayer in public schools? We don't have even that much prayer in many churches! Out of humility, you would think we would keep quiet on that particular subject until we practice what we preach in our own congregations.

I am sure that the Roman emperors didn't have prayer to God in their schools. But then, the early Christians didn't seem to care what Caligula or Claudius or Nero did. How could any emperor stop God? How, in fact, could the demons of hell make headway when God's people prayed and called upon his name? Impossible!

In the New Testament we don't see Peter or John wringing their hands and saying, "Oh, what are we going to do? Caligula's bisexual ... he wants to appoint his horse to the Roman Senate ... what a terrible model of leadership! How are we going to respond to this outrage?"

Let's not play games with ourselves. Let's not divert attention away from the weak prayer life of our own churches. In Acts 4, when the apostles were unjustly arrested, imprisoned, and threatened, they didn't call for a protest; they didn't reach for some political leverage. Instead, they headed to a prayer meeting. Soon the place was vibrating with the power of the Holy Spirit (vv. 23–31).

The apostles had this instinct: When in trouble, pray. When intimidated, pray. When challenged, pray. When persecuted, pray.

The British Bible translator J. B. Phillips, after completing his work on this section of Scripture, could not help reflecting on what he had observed. In the 1955 preface to his first edition of Acts, he wrote:

> It is impossible to spend several months in close study of the remarkable short book ... without being profoundly stirred and, to be honest, disturbed. The reader is stirred because he is seeing Christianity, the real thing, in action for the first time in human history. The newborn Church, as vulnerable as any human child, having neither money, influence nor power in the ordinary sense, is setting forth joyfully and courageously to win the pagan world for God through Christ....
>
> Yet we cannot help feeling disturbed as well as moved, for this surely is the Church as it was meant to be. It is vigorous and flexible, for these are the days before it ever became fat and short of breath through prosperity, or muscle-bound by overorganization. These men did not make 'acts of faith,' they believed; they did not 'say their prayers,' they really prayed. They did not hold conferences on psychosomatic medicine, they simply healed the sick. But if they were uncomplicated

and naive by modern standards, we have ruefully to admit that they were open on the God-ward side in a way that is almost unknown today.[1]

Open on the God-ward side ... doesn't that stir your spirit? That one brief phrase sums up the secret of power in the early church, a secret that hasn't changed one bit in twenty centuries.

No One Too Tough

A FASCINATING FOOTNOTE APPEARS in Acts 9 when Saul of Tarsus, the violent persecutor of the church, was converted, and God needed a believer to minister to him. Naturally, no Christian wanted to get within five blocks of the man. Yet God coaxed Ananias along by saying, "Go ... ask for a man from Tarsus named Saul, for he is praying" (v. 11). This was the proof, it seems, that everything had changed. "It's okay, Ananias ... calm down ... you don't have to be afraid now, it's safe: He's praying."

At the Brooklyn Tabernacle a few years ago, we saw the Lord break through to an equally tough sinner in answer to believing prayer. The whole outreach that touched Ricardo Aparicio was born in prayer.

Most ministries in our church have *not* begun with a bright idea in a pastors' meeting. We usually don't say, "Let's start a street outreach," and then go recruit laypeople to staff it. We have learned over the years to let God birth something in people who are spiritually sensitive, who begin to pray and feel a calling. Then they come to us. "We want to start such-and-such," they say—and the ministry gets going and lasts. Discouragement, complications, and other attacks by the enemy don't wash it out.

A fellow named Terry and some others grew concerned for the subculture of male prostitutes that flourishes on the Lower West Side of Manhattan in a place called the "salt mines," where the city keeps salt for deicing streets in the winter. This sick subculture ranges up to a couple of hundred men when the weather is warm. Living in abandoned vehicles or subterranean cavities, many dress in drag and offer themselves to customers who come by—some of them wealthy professionals in stretch limousines.

Many of them, as boys, were raped by adult male relatives. At the "salt mines" they start as young as age sixteen but they don't last much beyond forty; after that, they are either in jail or dead from a sexually transmitted disease or a drug overdose. The neighborhood has many leather-and-chain bars. Some of the male prostitutes carry razor blades for protection.

Our outreach team began to bring food and blankets during the daylight hours on Saturday, when the men weren't distracted by their "work." Although the men made considerable money, they tended to squander it on drugs. That left them scavenging garbage cans and dumpsters for food.

To feel compassion for these guys, to understand their wretched life, was extremely difficult. We prayed fervently on Tuesday nights for love, compassion—and protection.

My teenage daughter Susan became part of the team, and more than once she told me, "Daddy, it was so frustrating last night! I was talking to this drag queen about Jesus, and he was really listening to me. And just when I thought I was getting somewhere with him—up rolls this limo, the rear door opens a crack, a hand beckons—and he's gone. 'Sorry, Susan—gotta take care of business now,' he says to me."

All was not in vain, however. One Sunday afternoon about half an hour before the afternoon service, Terry knocked on my office door. "Pastor Cymbala! We've got twenty-seven guys here today from the 'salt mines.' Isn't that great!"

"How did that happen?" I asked.

"We got a bunch of vans and brought them. For many of them, this is going to be their first time ever in church."

I learned later that one of them had a machete inside the sleeve of his raincoat just "in case" he felt he needed to use it.

The congregation took their presence in stride, even though the men didn't exactly look—or smell—All-American. At the end of the service some of them responded to give their hearts to the Lord. Others sat stunned as church members greeted them with smiles and handshakes.

Walking down the center aisle, I bumped into an attractive woman in a black dress, with blond, shoulder-length hair, nicely done nails, black stockings, and high heels. "Excuse me, ma'am," I said.

She turned ... and this low voice with a heavy Spanish accent replied, "No, that's okay, man."

My heart skipped a beat. This was not a woman after all. But neither was it a sloppy transvestite. This was a knockout of a "woman"—bone-thin, no body hair thanks to hormonal treatment. As I took closer notice, the only visual giveaway was the Adam's apple.

I edged toward my wife. "Carol, you're not going to believe this," I whispered, "but that's a *guy* standing over there."

"Don't fool me," she said.

"I'm not kidding. That *is* a guy—trust me."

His name was Ricardo, known on the street as "Sarah." Terry reported later, "He was the main troublemaker of all. He introduced all the young kids to crack cocaine and prostitution." Ricardo had been plying his trade for at least ten years, and the dreariness was finally starting to get to him. Imagine the despair of hustling most of the night to make

$400 or $600, immediately blowing that money on cocaine, falling asleep under a bridge ... and waking up the next morning to pick through garbage cans looking for some breakfast. The next night, as evening draws near, you start all over again.

Ricardo sat in the meetings, and it dawned on him that maybe he *could* be different. This Jesus could actually set him free from crack. Perhaps this Jesus could even change him into a true man, not this half-and-half person he assumed was his nature. He had been teased from childhood about being effeminate. His mother had pleaded with him to forsake homosexuality, and he had tried, to no avail. His willpower had failed him countless times.

But the idea that God was stronger, that God could in fact change him on the inside ... that was a new thought. Ricardo kept listening, and after about a month, he gave his heart to the Lord. It was not a dramatic conversion; I am not even sure when it happened. But it was real on the inside.

I will never forget the Tuesday night we introduced him to the congregation. He stood before us, a bit shy, in male clothing. His blond hair had been cut, and dark roots were now growing out. His nail polish had been chipped off. Subconscious habits were being overhauled with instruction from Terry and the others: "No, Ricardo, don't cross your legs like that. Put your ankle all the way up on your other knee...." It sounds humorous, but they had to start all the way back at "square one" with how a man sits and walks.

The congregation couldn't help but cheer and praise God for this miracle. Ricardo stood there perplexed at the noise. Why were all these people applauding him?

In the months that followed, Ricardo made great progress in his spiritual life. It took three months to get him straight enough even to be accepted in a drug rehabilitation program. Nevertheless, his commitment to follow Christ was solid. The old had gone, the new had definitely come.

Ricardo had come out of pitch blackness and into the light. Charles Spurgeon once said that when a jeweler shows his best diamonds, he sets them against a black velvet backdrop. The contrast of the jewels against the dark velvet brings out the luster. In the same way, God does his most stunning work where things seem hopeless. Wherever there is pain, suffering, and desperation, Jesus is. And that's where his people belong—among those who are vulnerable, who think nobody cares. What better place for the brilliance of Christ to shine?

Ricardo eventually moved to Texas. I was in Dallas one summer and ran into him. It was great to see the transformation. He had gained weight and was every inch a real man. I hugged him, and then he delivered a new shock:

"Pastor, I wish you could come back in two weeks. I'm getting married!"

"You're what?" My mind flashed back to the first time I had met him dressed in drag.

"Oh, yes," he said. "I've met a Christian woman named Betty, and we love each other deeply. We're getting married."

The fact that Ricardo had AIDS made the situation complicated. But with proper guidance and counseling, he and Betty established a new home together.

A Legacy to Leave

A few years later, at Christmastime, while I was in my office just as the Sunday afternoon service was beginning, I received a message that said Ricardo was dying. He wanted to talk to me.

I slumped in my chair, and as I picked up the phone, Betty's voice greeted me. "Hello, Pastor. . . . When I put my husband on the phone, you won't be able to hear much, because he's very weak. But he still remembers all that you and the church did for him."

In a moment I heard a fragile, wispy voice say, "Pastor—Cymbala—so—glad—to—hear—you."

I choked up.

Ricardo continued, forcing out the breathy syllables: "I—never—forgot—how—you—all—loved—me—and—took—me—in.—Thank—you—so—much."

My ministerial instincts then revived, and I prepared to make a comforting little speech, to tell him he would be going to heaven soon, that he would get there before me but I would see him on the other side for all eternity. . . .

The Holy Spirit stopped me. *No!* a voice seemed to say. *Fight for him! Cry out to me!*

I changed course. "Ricardo, I'm going to pray for you right now. Don't try to pray along with me; save your strength." I began to intercede with intensity, fighting against the death that loomed before him. "O God, touch Ricardo with your power! This is *not* his time to die. Restore him, for your glory, I pray." I remember even hitting my desk a couple of times with my fist.

When I finished, I marched directly into the meeting and stopped it. "I've just gotten off the phone with Ricardo, whom most of you know," I said. People looked up expectantly all across the building. "He's very sick with AIDS—but I want us to pray for his recovery."

That unleashed a torrent of prayer as people cried out to God for Ricardo.

I called Betty two days later. "Pastor Cymbala, it's incredible!" she reported. "He went to sleep after the two of you talked—and the next day, all his vital signs had done a U-turn. He began to eat, after taking almost nothing for days."

Within three weeks, Ricardo actually flew to New York and came walking unannounced into a Tuesday night prayer meeting. The crowd gasped with joy.

In my heart I felt that God spared him for a reason: To get his testimony onto video so that others could know his remarkable story. This eventually became a gripping eight-minute segment of the Brooklyn Tabernacle Choir's concert video called *Live at Madison Square Garden* (Warner Alliance). The power of his testimony, shot on the streets in the "salt mines," is riveting. It may partly explain why the video surprised us all by staying on *Billboard*'s national best-seller list for months.

The last time I saw Ricardo, a year later, his weight had dropped again. "I'm so tired," he said. "I've fought this disease long enough; I just want to go to Jesus. I can go now, because you have me on film, and everybody will know in years to come what Jesus did in my life." He passed away not long afterward.

THE SECRET OF GRACE

RICARDO'S STORY IS EVIDENCE of what God will do in response to fervent prayer. No one is beyond his grace. No situation, anywhere on earth, is too hard for God.

The apostle Paul, having benefited from that grace in his own life, preached and wrote about it ever after. He outlines in Romans 10:13–15 a chain of events that describes New Testament salvation:

> "Everyone who calls on the name of the Lord will be saved." How, then, can they call on the one they have not believed in? And how can they believe in the one of whom they have not heard? And how can they hear

without someone preaching to them? And how can they preach unless they are sent?

Churches often refer to this passage in connection with overseas missionary work. "We need to give a good offering today in order to send out preachers," they say—which is true. But that is just the beginning of Paul's sequence.

Sending leads to *preaching*.

Preaching leads to *hearing*.

Hearing leads to *believing*.

Believing leads to *calling on the name of the Lord*.

Notice that believing is not the climax. Even the great Protestant Reformers who taught us the principle of *sola fide* ("faith alone") also preached that intellectual assent alone does not bring salvation. There is one more step for demonstrating a real and living faith, and that is calling out to God with all of one's heart and soul.

The clearest instructions about church life come in the Pastoral Letters, where Paul tells young pastors such as Timothy how to proceed. The apostle couldn't be more direct than in 1 Timothy 2:1:

"I urge then, first of all, that requests, prayers, intercession and thanksgiving be made for everyone."

Why? Why first of all, before anything else? *Well, Timothy my son, we've got to remember that God's house is to be called a house of prayer.*

Later in the same chapter (v. 8), Paul says, "I want men everywhere to lift up holy hands in prayer, without anger or disputing." That is the sign of a Christian church.

The book of Revelation says that when the twenty-four elders eventually fall at the feet of Jesus, each one will have a golden bowl—and do you know what's in the bowls? What is this incense that is so fragrant to Christ? "The prayers of the saints" (Rev. 5:8).

Just imagine … you and I kneel or stand or sit down to pray, really opening our hearts to God—and what we say is so precious to him that he keeps it like a treasure.

In the community where you live, what church do you know that takes a prominent night of the week, with all the leaders present, and says that because prayer is so great, so central to Jesus' definition of the church, they're going to concentrate on prayer?

Americans designate one day a year as a National Day of Prayer. Do we have any right to ask mayors and senators to show up for a special event, with the television cameras rolling, if we don't have regular prayer meetings in our churches? If praying is that important, why don't we do it every week?

How is it that Christians today will pay $20 to hear the latest Christian artist in concert, but Jesus can't draw a crowd?

For myself, I have decided that the Tuesday night prayer meeting is so crucial that I will never be out of town two Tuesdays in a row. If that means I can't accept certain speaking invitations across the land, so be it. Why would I prefer to be anywhere else?

The Bible has all these promises:

"Ask and it will be given to you; seek and you will find; knock and the door will be opened to you" (Matt. 7:7).

"You will seek me and find me when you seek me with all your heart" (Jer. 29:13).

"You do not have, because you do not ask God" (James 4:2).

Isn't it time to say, "Stop! We're going to pray, because God said that when we pray, he will intervene."

The sad truth is, in the city where I live—as in Chicago and Philadelphia and Houston and right across to L.A.—

more people are turning to crack than to Christ. More people are dipping into drugs than are getting baptized in water. What is going to reverse this tide? Preaching alone will not do it; classes aren't going to do it; more money for more programs won't do it. Only turning God's house into a house of fervent prayer will reverse the power of evil so evident in the world today.

> **More people are turning to crack than to Christ. More people are dipping into drugs than are getting baptized in water.** ❧

THE MISSING LINK

OVER THE LAST 30 years, more books have been written about marriage than in all the preceding 2,000 years of church history. But ask any pastor in America if there aren't proportionally more troubled marriages today than in any other era. We have all the how-to's, but homes are still falling apart.

The couple that prays together stays together. I don't mean to be simplistic; there will be difficult moments in any union. But God's Word is true when it says, "Call upon me, and I will help you. Just give me a chance."

The same holds true for parenting. We may own stacks of good books on child rearing and spending "quality time" with our children. Yet we have more problems per 100 young people in the church today than at any previous time. This is not because we lack knowledge or how-to; it is because we have not cried out for the power and grace of God.

What if, in the last 25 years, we had invested only half the time and energy in writing, publishing, reading, and discussing books on the Christian family ... and put the other half into praying for our marriages and our children? I am certain we would be in far better shape today.

Again, J. B. Phillips points out with great insight:

> The Holy Spirit has a way of short-circuiting human problems. Indeed, in exactly the same way as Jesus Christ in the flesh cut right through the matted layers of tradition and exposed the real issue; ... so we find here [in Acts] the Spirit of Jesus dealing not so much with problems as with people. Many problems comparable to modern complexities never arise here because the men and women concerned were of one heart and mind in the Spirit.... Since God's Holy Spirit cannot conceivably have changed one iota through the centuries, ... He is perfectly prepared to short-circuit, by an inflow of love, wisdom and understanding, many human problems today.[2]

That is why the writer to the Hebrews nails down the most central activity of all for Christians: "Let us then approach the throne of grace with confidence, so that we may receive mercy and find grace to help us in our time of need" (Heb. 4:16). It doesn't say, "Let us come to the sermon." We in America have made the sermon the centerpiece of the church, something God never intended. Preachers who are really doing their job get people to come to the throne of grace. That's the true source of grace and mercy.

To every preacher and every singer, God will someday ask, "Did you bring people to where the action could be found ... at the throne of grace? If you just entertained them, if you just tickled their ears and gave them a warm, fuzzy moment, woe unto you. At the throne of grace, I could have changed their lives. Jim Cymbala, did you just dazzle people with your cleverness, or did you make them hungry to come to me?"

If a meeting doesn't end with people touching God, what kind of a meeting is it? We haven't really encountered God. We haven't met with the only One powerful and loving enough to change our lives.

I am well aware that we don't get everything we ask for; we have to ask according to God's will. But let us not use theological dodges to avoid the fact that we often go without things God wants us to have right now, today, because we fail to ask. Too seldom do we get honest enough to admit, "Lord, I can't handle this alone. I've just hit the wall for the thirty-second time and *I need you*."

The words of the old hymn ring true:

> Oh, what peace we often forfeit,
> Oh, what needless pain we bear,
> All because we do not carry
> Everything to God in prayer.

God has chosen prayer as his channel of blessing. He has spread a table for us with every kind of wisdom, grace, and strength because he knows exactly what we need. But the only way we can get it is to pull up to the table and taste and see that the Lord is good.

Pulling up to that table is called the prayer of faith.

In other words, God doesn't tell us to pray because he wants to impose some sort of regimen on us. This is not a system of legalism. E. M. Bounds wrote,

> Prayer ought to enter into the spiritual habits, but it ceases to be prayer when it is carried on by habit only.... Desire gives fervor to prayer. The soul cannot be listless when some great desire fixes and inflames it.... Strong desires make strong prayers....

The neglect of prayer is the fearful token of dead spiritual desires. The soul has turned away from God when desire after him no longer presses it into the closet. There can be no true praying without desire.[3]

God says to us, "Pray, because I have all kinds of things for you; and when you ask, you will receive. I have all this grace, and you live with scarcity. Come unto me, all you who labor. Why are you so rushed? Where are you running *now?* Everything you need, I have."

If the times are indeed as bad as we say they are . . . if the darkness in our world is growing heavier by the moment . . . if we are facing spiritual battles right in our own homes and churches . . . then we are foolish not to turn to the One who supplies unlimited grace and power. He is our only source. We are crazy to ignore him.

PART 2

Diversions from God's Best

SIX

A Time for Shaking

IMAGINE YOURSELF AT MADISON Square Garden for a college basketball game on a January night back in the mid-1960s. The Rhode Island Rams, my team, have come down to New York to play, say, Fordham or St. John's. You take your seat down close to the floor a few minutes before the opening tip-off.

After eight or nine minutes, the Rams are losing 23 to 7. We're committing foolish turnovers, we're not rebounding aggressively, we're giving up fast breaks.

The coach calls a time-out. We huddle, and one player says, "Isn't this fun? We get to play in Madison Square Garden!"

Another says, "I really like the gold trim here on the uniforms. Looks sharp against the white, doesn't it?"

A third is waving to his Aunt Nellie up in the mezzanine seats, while a fourth runs over to plant a quick kiss on his girlfriend's cheek.

If this had actually happened, what do you think Coach Calverley would have said to us? "Hey! Would you guys please look at the scoreboard? We're getting killed! When you go back out there, I want you to go into a tight man-to-man press, in the backcourt as well as up front. No more sleepwalking! This game is going to get away from us if you guys don't wake up!"

Actually, he wouldn't have said it that politely.

As a team we couldn't fantasize or make believe we were doing well. The scoreboard was the inescapable signal that we had to change our game plan.

The Christian world today is not playing nearly as well as we think. We are often confusing faith with fantasy. Although Hebrews 11:6 declares that "without faith it is impossible to please God," we seem to have grown adept at putting a positive spin on every conceivable situation. "These are wonderful days!" some preachers exult. "What a great time of blessing for God's people."

Meanwhile, Christian researcher George Barna reports that 64 percent of "born-again" Americans and 40 percent of "evangelical" Americans say there is no such thing as absolute truth. In other words, the Ten Commandments may or may not be valid, Jesus Christ isn't necessarily the only way to God, and so forth. With this kind of sloppy thinking, what does "born again" even mean anymore? In the rush for "success" and "growth," we have revised and distorted the very essence of the gospel.

More than three-fourths of current church growth, Barna adds, is merely "transfer growth"—people moving from one church to another. Despite all the Christian broadcasting and high-profile campaigns, the Christian population is not growing in numbers nationally. In fact, church attendance in a given week during 1996 was down to 37 percent of the population, a ten-year low . . . even though 82 percent of Americans claim to be Christians.

Yet everyone agrees that the culture is becoming more promiscuous, more violent, and more hateful by the day. So what has happened to the church as light and salt in the earth? What do spin doctors in the body of Christ make of these things?

WELCOME TO LAODICEA

I SAY WE ARE in trouble. It is high time to wake up and look at the scoreboard.

With some exceptions, we are like the church at Laodicea. In fact, we have so institutionalized Laodiceanism that we think lukewarm is normal. Any church winning more than a few people to Christ is considered "outstanding."

We are like the church at Laodicea. In fact, we have so institutionalized Laodiceanism that we think lukewarm is normal. ❧

The stern words of Jesus apply to us as much as to Christians at the end of the first century: "You are neither cold nor hot. I wish you were either one or the other! So, because you are lukewarm—neither hot nor cold—I am about to spit you out of my mouth. You say, 'I am rich; I have acquired wealth and do not need a thing'" (Rev. 3:15–17). In other words, they were voicing a wonderful "positive confession." They were proclaiming victory and blessing. The only trouble is, Jesus was unimpressed. He responded:

"But you do not realize that you are wretched, pitiful, poor, blind and naked. . . . Those whom I love I rebuke and discipline. So be earnest, and repent" (Rev. 3:17, 19).

Strong language, to be sure. Jesus always deals strongly, however, with those he loves. "What son is not disciplined by his father?" asks the writer of Hebrews (12:7).

Notice that the Laodiceans were saints of God, with all the promises to claim. They were part of Christ's body— singing hymns, worshiping on Sunday, enjoying physical benefits, and no doubt viewing themselves as more righteous than their pagan neighbors. Yet they were on the verge of being vomited out. What a wake-up call!

THE FIRST FACE-OFF

WHENEVER THE BODY OF Christ gets into trouble—whether through its own negligence, as in Laodicea, or through some special attack of Satan—strong action is required. We cannot merely sit by and hope the problem will resolve itself.

We can benefit from studying what the early church did when it got into trouble.

The disciples had enjoyed three years of teaching from Jesus. They had been discipled by the Master Discipler. But mere teaching is never enough, even if it comes directly from Jesus. Because they did not have the empowerment of the Holy Spirit, the disciples acted like cowards on the night of Jesus' arrest.

Once they were empowered on the Day of Pentecost, however, they became the church victorious, the church militant. With the gracious manifestation of God's Spirit in the Upper Room, the disciples encountered their first audience. Peter, the biggest failure of them all, became the preacher that day. It was no homiletical masterpiece, to be sure. But people were deeply convicted—"cut to the heart," according to Acts 2:37—by his anointed words. Three thousand were gathered into the church that day.

Which church? Baptist? Presbyterian? Pentecostal? There were no such labels at that time—and in God's view of things, there still aren't. He ignores our categories. All he sees when he looks down is the body of Christ, made up of all born-again, blood-washed believers. The only subdivisions he sees are geographical—local churches. Other distinctions are immaterial.

I find it curious that we Christians will vigorously defend what Ephesians 4 says about "one Lord" (no polytheism) and "one faith" (salvation through Christ alone) ... but then grow strangely silent regarding "one body" (vv. 4–6). At that point we start making excuses, historical and otherwise, for the shameful divisions within the church.

The early Christians began dynamically in power. They were unified, prayerful, filled with the Holy Spirit, going out to do God's work in God's way, and seeing results that glorified him. The hour seemed golden. This was truly the church overcoming the gates of hell, as Jesus described.

One day a public miracle occurred—the healing of the lame man, as related in Acts 3—which drew another crowd, and another sermon from Peter. Thousands more believed in Christ.

Then came the first attack. The priests, Sadducees, and captain of the temple guard broke in on them "greatly disturbed because the apostles were teaching the people and proclaiming in Jesus the resurrection of the dead. They seized Peter and John, and because it was evening, they put them in jail until the next day" (Acts 4:2–3).

Jesus had warned that difficult days would come. Now they were here. Although the attacks later on would come in the form of false teaching or internal division, this blow was physical and frontal.

A surprise awaited the Jewish leaders, however. "When they saw the courage of Peter and John and realized that they were unschooled, ordinary men, they were astonished and they took note that these men had been with Jesus" (4:13). These fishermen seemed guileless, sincere—quite the opposite of what we so often see today, which results in a great deal more polish in the pulpit, and a great deal less power.

The apostles were released on the condition that they not speak further in the name of Jesus. How did they respond? What did they do?

They didn't petition the government. They didn't wring their hands about how unfair this was. They didn't complain about losing their freedom of speech, although they could have made a solid case that the Roman Empire, with its panoply of other gods, shouldn't mind their speaking about the god named Jesus. The apostles could have done any number of things to sway public opinion. But to their minds this was not a political problem—it was spiritual. They quickly joined a meeting of the believers and began to pray. They immediately turned to their primitive power source.

This is how they prayed:

> "Sovereign Lord, . . . you made the heaven and the earth and the sea, and everything in them. . . . Now, Lord, consider their threats and enable your servants to speak your word with great boldness. Stretch out your hand to heal and perform miraculous signs and wonders through the name of your holy servant Jesus" (Acts 4:24, 29–30).

This is precisely what the prophets, down through the centuries, had told them to do: When under attack, when facing a new challenge, in all seasons, in all times, call on the name of the Lord, and he will help you.

It sounds as if things got rather energetic, perhaps even a little noisy: "They raised their voices together in prayer to God" (v. 24). When we read such passages, it is important not to force them into the context of our particular tradition. Would you or I have felt comfortable in the room that day? It doesn't matter. This is the church on the move, giving us a Spirit-inspired model for today.

This is the only prayer longer than a sentence or two that is quoted in the entire book of Acts. No doubt it is only a summary of what the group prayed in a variety of words that day. Yet it offers a unique glimpse at the prayer life of the early church. As seriously as we revere and study the long prayer of Jesus in the garden (John 17), we should also examine what is said here.

Isn't it strange that the group prayed for boldness? We might have expected them to pray, "Lord, help us find a safe shelter now. We need to 'lie low' for a few weeks until the heat goes away. We'll stay out of sight, and if you could just make the Sanhedrin sort of forget about us ..."

Not at all. If anything, they prayed against backing down. They asked God to help them press on. Retreat was the furthest thing from their minds.

And how did God react?

"After they prayed, the place where they were meeting was shaken. And they were all filled with the Holy Spirit and spoke the word of God boldly" (v. 31).

The first time vocalist Steve Green came to sing at the Brooklyn Tabernacle, we gathered in my office with the associate pastors to pray just before the meeting began. We prayed in unison that God would come among us that day.

When we opened our eyes, Steve had an odd look on his face. "What was that vibration I just felt?" he asked. "Is there a train that runs near here, or was that really ...?"

I explained that, as far as I knew, the rumble wasn't caused by the power of the Holy Spirit—would to God it was! Rather, it was the passing of the "D" train in the subway that runs directly beneath our building.

For the early church that day in Jerusalem, however, the vibration was nothing short of Spirit-induced. In that prayer meeting God's power came in a fresh, new, deeper way.

96 ✒ FRESH WIND, FRESH FIRE

These people had already been filled with the Holy Spirit on the Day of Pentecost (Acts 2), but here they sensed a new need. God met them with a new infusion of power.

I am well aware that Christians disagree today on whether the infilling (baptism, empowerment) of the Spirit is a part of the salvation "package" or a separate, subsequent experience. Long and intense discussions go on about that. Whatever you or I believe, let us admit that this passage shows bona fide Christians experiencing a fresh infilling. The apostles didn't claim they already had everything they needed. Now that they were under attack, they received fresh power, fresh courage, fresh fire from the Holy Spirit.

Our store of spiritual power apparently dissipates with time. Daily living, distractions, and spiritual warfare take their toll. We need, in the words Paul used in Ephesians 5:18, to "be always being filled with the Spirit" (literal translation).

> **Can anyone say with a straight face that the Laodiceans, at the time Jesus addressed them in the letter, had a Spirit-filled church?** ✒

Positional theology is good as far as it goes, such as "I am God's child regardless of how I feel at the moment." But if we stretch this idea to make statements such as "I am categorically Spirit-filled for the rest of my life," we deceive ourselves.

Can anyone say with a straight face that the Laodiceans, at the time Jesus addressed them in the letter, had a Spirit-filled church? They were Christians, to be sure. But they were in desperate need of an Acts 4-type prayer meeting.

Andrew Bonar wrote in his diary on December 13, 1880, "I long more and more to be filled with the Spirit, and to see my congregation moved and melted under the Word, as in great revival times, 'the place shaken where they are assembled together,' because the Lord has come in power."[1]

Whether we call ourselves classical evangelicals, traditionalists, fundamentalists, Pentecostals, or charismatics, we all have to face our lack of real power and call out for a fresh infilling of the Spirit. We need the fresh wind of God to awaken us from our lethargy. We must not hide any longer behind some theological argument. The days are too dark and dangerous.

STRAIGHT AHEAD

THE WORK OF GOD can only be carried on by the power of God. The church is a spiritual organism fighting spiritual battles. Only spiritual power can make it function as God ordained.

The key is not money, organization, cleverness, or education. Are you and I seeing the results Peter saw? Are we bringing thousands of men and women to Christ the way he did? If not, we need to get back to his power source. No matter the society or culture, the city or town, God has never lacked the power to work through available people to glorify his name.

> **Are you and I seeing the results Peter saw? If not, we need to get back to his power source. ❧**

When we sincerely turn to God, we will find that his church always moves *forward*, not *backward*. We can never back up and accommodate ourselves to what the world wants or expects. Our stance must remain militant, aggressive, bold.

That is what characterized General William Booth and the early Salvation Army as they invaded the slums of

London. It characterized the early mission movements, such as the Moravians. It characterized Hudson Taylor in China as well as revivalists on the American frontier. These Christians were not bulls in a china shop, but they did speak the truth in love—fearlessly.

In the familiar story of David and Goliath, there is a wonderful moment when the giant gets irked at the sight of his young opponent. "Am I a dog, that you come at me with sticks?" he roars (1 Sam. 17:43). Goliath is genuinely insulted. "Come here, . . . and I'll give your flesh to the birds of the air and the beasts of the field!" (v. 44).

Does David flinch? Does he opt for a strategic retreat behind some tree or boulder, thinking maybe to buy a little time?

Absolutely not.

"As the Philistine moved closer to attack him, *David ran quickly toward the battle line to meet him*" (v. 48).

That is the picture of what God wants for us today: *running toward the fray!*

David's weaponry was ridiculous: a sling and five stones. It didn't matter. God still uses foolish tools in the hands of weak people to build his kingdom. Backed by prayer and his power, we can accomplish the unthinkable.

The Brooklyn Tabernacle Choir sings a song that captures God's penchant for using the weak to shame the strong. It goes, "If you can use anything, Lord, you can use me." Kenneth Ware, one of the associate pastors, has shown this kind of faith more than once. Years ago, this godly, gray-haired African American started all-night prayer meetings on Friday nights in the church. Then he organized a Prayer Band—a group of people committed to calling on the Lord at the church on a continuing schedule.

Soon the members of the Prayer Band were praying five nights a week, from 11 P.M. to 6 A.M. Today they are in the church seven days a week, twenty-four hours a day, praying in three-hour shifts or longer. Every request we receive is written on a little card and lifted to the Lord for the next thirty days.

I remember the day Pastor Ware said to me in a fatherly tone (he's at least fifteen years older than I am), "Pastor, you know, we're still not seeing God do all he wants to do. You're preaching with all your heart, but we need to see more conviction of sin, more of God's manifest presence in our services."

I agreed and listened, wondering what he would say next.

"I'm serious," Pastor Ware continued. "We probably have half a dozen HIV-positive people in every meeting. We've got crack addicts. We've got marriages on the rocks, brokenhearted moms, young people hardened by the city. They really need the Lord.

"I want to have the Prayer Band start praying somewhere about this *during* the actual meetings, while you're preaching. We need to see God break through among us."

I gave Pastor Ware my blessing, and to this day he has twenty or so people closed in a room to pray during each of the four meetings—a total of eighty intercessors each Sunday. They start by praying with the pastors fifteen minutes before the meeting and keep going even after everything ends. Sometimes, in leaving the building at ten or ten-thirty at night, I have heard them still praying.

The first or second Sunday of this effort, I was in my office getting ready for the afternoon service when I heard, through the heating ducts, a noise from the room upstairs . . . the sound of people praying. The worship had just begun, and the Prayer Band was already calling on God.

Someone must have been kneeling at a chair directly beside a vent, because I distinctly heard a woman's voice say: "God, protect him. Help him, Lord. Use him to proclaim your Word today. Convict of sin; change people, Lord!"

My heart started to beat faster. My spirit began to rise toward the throne of grace along with theirs. In a few minutes I left my office wondering what God might have in store for us that afternoon.

The place was packed as usual. The choir sang, and I preached with all my heart about the love of God. "How desperately God wants you to come to him," I pleaded near the end. "What damns a soul in the end and sends you off into a terrible eternity is rejecting the love of God. He chases you, tries to hem you in, tries to get your attention. This love, this passion for you, is so real. He desires the death of no one. He wants everyone to come to a knowledge of the truth. Don't reject God's love! Don't go there! That's what will seal your doom."

As I reached the end of my message, I moved to the side of the pulpit and closed my eyes. I kept urging people to come to the front and respond to God's love. I kept talking, lost in my passion for those who didn't know Christ. . . .

....

What I didn't see, because I had my eyes shut, was the steel-gray 38-caliber revolver in the man's right hand, leveled right at me. ❧

....

A Jewish man about 25 years old, wearing beige chinos and a light green sport shirt, stood up in the back row of the lower auditorium and began edging toward the center aisle. What I didn't see, because I still had my eyes shut, was the steel-gray 38-caliber revolver in his right hand, leveled at me!

Down the aisle he came, the gun pointed right at my chest. Many in the congregation didn't notice because their eyes, like mine, were closed. The ones who saw him froze in terror. Even the ushers seemed paralyzed. By the time they sprang into action, it was too late—the man was coming up the steps onto the platform. All the while, I continued to implore the crowd to yield to God's love, having no idea that my life seemed in imminent danger.

Carol was playing the piano behind me, and her eyes were wide open. In panic she screamed my name twice: "Jim! Jim!" I didn't hear her. I was busy urging people to come to Jesus—and seemingly, I was on my way to Jesus myself right then.

Carol was sure she was about to witness the cold-blooded murder of her husband—and then what? Would the fellow turn on her next?

He did neither. Instead, he walked up right beside me and tossed the weapon onto the pulpit. Suddenly I heard a crash, my eyes flew open—*and there's a gun on my pulpit!*

The man started to run back across the platform, down the steps, and up the aisle again. My only instinct was to chase after him and call, "No, no—don't go! It's okay. Wait!—"

He fell into a heap and began to weep as he cried out in a pitiful moan, "Jesus, help me! I can't take it anymore!"

By then the ushers were on top of him, not to harm him but to control the situation and also to begin to pray for him. Meanwhile, the church was in pandemonium. Some people were crying, others were praying aloud, still others sat in stunned silence.

In a moment I walked back up to the pulpit. I took a deep breath, then held up the gun—not realizing it was loaded—and said just one sentence, more to myself than to the audience:

"Look what the love of God can make somebody give up."

Suddenly, from all over the building, people began to race to the altar. God had attached the final point to my message. A great harvest of needy souls came to the loving Christ that day.

As I watched the response, my mind went back to the woman's prayer a couple of hours earlier: "Lord, protect him today. Convict of sin; change lives. . . ."

The man, somewhat unbalanced in his mind, said he had never intended to hurt me. He was planning to hurt somebody who had meddled with his girlfriend . . . and he had just stopped by our meeting on the way. He became so convicted of the hate in his heart that he said to himself, *I have to get rid of this gun. I must give it to the preacher.*

As a result of the Prayer Band's praying straight into the face of danger, a life was spared. A great victory for God's kingdom was won; we baptized more than a dozen people as a result of that one meeting. The power of God was evident, and his work went forward.

THE FALLOUT

WHILE MOST PEOPLE WERE relieved and rejoicing at the outcome, my wife was in shock. She said very little the rest of that Sunday. The next morning, as we were having coffee, she let go of her feelings.

"Is that the way it's going to end for us someday, Jim? Is that how we're going to go out—somebody's just going to walk up and kill you in a meeting?

"We have no protection up there! Where were the ushers? Where were the security people? We could easily have been killed yesterday."

I tried to console her and reason with her. "No, Carol— the Lord protected us this time, and he will in the future.

The ushers had no chance to stop him anyway." But my words fell flat.

All week long, Carol suffered. The fear was oppressive. She had trouble sleeping. I would find her staring into space, replaying the awful moments of Sunday afternoon in her mind, again and again.

That Friday night Carol made herself lead the choir practice as usual. Following their custom, the members began with a half hour or more of prayer and worship before ever singing a note.

The Holy Spirit spoke to one of the choir members. She came out of her section to stand beside Carol, took the microphone, and said, "You know what? I believe God just showed me that we should lift up Carol in prayer. Would you all join me?"

They gathered around, laid hands on my wife, and began to pray with intensity. In that moment, something happened that five days of her brooding and my consoling had not achieved. Carol was free of fear once again.

When we get serious about drawing upon God's power, remarkable things will happen. Even if we grow listless and lukewarm, still Christ says, "Here I am! I stand at the door and knock. If anyone hears my voice and opens the door, I will come and eat with him, and he with me.... He who has an ear, let him hear what the Spirit says to the churches" (Rev. 3:20, 22).

Those gentle words, quoted often by evangelists to those who do not know Christ, were addressed to the Laodicean Christians whom Jesus had just scolded. Although he was grieved by their lethargy, he nevertheless offered his renewing love and power to any who would open the door. Will we?

SEVEN

The Lure of Novelty

IN THE WORLD OF advertising, every copywriter knows the power of two magic words: "Free!" and "New!" We see them in the supermarket, in the newspaper, on billboards. And consumers respond.

In the church today, we are falling prey to the appeal of "New!" The old truths of the gospel don't seem spectacular enough. We're restless for the latest, greatest, newest teaching or technique. We pastors in particular seem to search for a short-cut or some dynamic new strategy that will fire up our churches.

The prayer of the early believers recorded in Acts 4 highlights three fundamentals from which we are in danger of sliding away: "Enable your servants to speak your word . . . with great boldness . . . Stretch out your hand to heal and per-form miraculous signs and wonders" (vv. 29–30).

I want to probe the first of these: "Enable your servants to speak your word. . . ."

There was no confusion in the minds of the first Chris-tians about *what* to proclaim. There was no searching for new and novel messages. The plain gospel that they heard from Jesus their Lord was considered entirely adequate.

I received a surprise at a large conference not long ago when, between sessions, I sat casually talking with a number of the other speakers. The conversation led to various emphases in the church today. Soon I found myself wonder-ing what religion they were discussing.

One man said how important it is for all believers to find out if any of their ancestors had ever attended a séance, even centuries ago. Unless that "generational curse" was removed we could not expect to prosper as Christians. Even our children and grandchildren would continue to be at risk, he claimed. Imagine being saved, a new creation in Christ, "rescued ... from the dominion of darkness and brought ... into the kingdom of the Son" (Col. 1:13)—yet somehow still under a curse of Satan!

I thought of the numerous Haitians at the Brooklyn Tabernacle who have come to New York from a land where the main religion is voodoo. If this man's teaching is true, these Haitians have a lot of homework to do, finding out which of their great-grandmothers had dabbled in the occult, then taking steps to break this long-standing bondage.

Why, I wondered, didn't Paul speak about this more clearly in his letters? The first century saw plenty of witchcraft. Did the believers in Corinth and Galatia and Rome have to explore their family trees for traces of an evil spell?

In one of the teaching sessions another speaker said, "There are three levels of spiritual warfare: battles with ordinary demons every day, confrontations with the occult such as astrology or New Age, and then strategic-level territorial warfare against the spirits in charge of a whole region. And even the apostle Paul never understood this third level or exercised this kind of ministry." Imagine this clever teacher transcending the great apostle of the New Testament!

I couldn't help wondering, what is the name of the demon over Brooklyn? The effects of evil are obvious enough on every street corner. Could I really knock the evil out with one rebuke of the territorial power over the whole borough?

Where does the New Testament portray this strategy? Did Peter bind the spirit over Joppa or Caesarea? Paul spent three years in Ephesus, a center of idol worship, yet there is no mention of "binding the spirit of the goddess Diana," whose temple in that city was one of the Seven Wonders of the Ancient World. In Acts 4, the apostles did not ask for the name of the evil spirit over Jerusalem.

Carol and I returned to the hotel sad and depressed. How tragic that young ministers were feverishly writing down all these exotic teachings in the vain hope of igniting their struggling churches back home with techniques and teachings nowhere found in Scripture.

I could find no evidence that these speakers were implementing their concepts at the local church level. Their books and tapes were selling well, but I wondered why they hadn't come to Brooklyn or other dark places and put their teachings into practice.

> **What we have today is the work of "technicians"
> or "revisionists" or "idea men" who feel the need
> to innovate, to devise novelties in order to help
> God's kingdom along.** ❦

I fear that what we have here is the work of "technicians" or "revisionists" or "idea men" who feel the need to innovate, to devise novelties in order to help God's kingdom along. Unfortunately, America's moral climate and the church's spiritual temperature prove these novelties to be impotent.

THE DEVIL IS STILL IN BUSINESS

IF PRESENT-DAY TEACHERS AND authors have in fact discovered something new under the theological sun, I have a question to ask:

Why is there still so much evil rampant in the earth if the devil has indeed been "bound" so many times by Christians today? One well-known preacher went to San Francisco a few years ago, rented a stadium, and did "spiritual warfare" for the night, claiming to bind and rebuke every evil spirit and principality in the city. The next day he and his entourage flew home again. Is San Francisco a more godly place today as a result?

The Bible speaks more about *resisting* the devil than it does about *binding* him. First Peter 5:8–9 says, "Your enemy the devil prowls around like a roaring lion looking for someone to devour. Resist him, standing firm in the faith, because you know that your brothers throughout the world are undergoing the same kind of sufferings." Why didn't the apostle Peter just *bind* that roaring lion and be done with the problem?

> **The Bible speaks more about *resisting* the devil than it does about *binding* him.** ❧

Jesus did talk in Matthew 12:29 about binding the strong man in order to rob his house. He used this metaphor immediately after casting a demon out of a blind and mute man. The meaning is that one person had been set free; nothing more cosmic in scope is mentioned. The text conveys that a strong man, Satan, had been evicted by a stronger one, Christ.

A similar truth can be applied to the practice of seeking to know a demon's name. Out of Jesus' dozens of encounters with Satan during his ministry, he asked for a name only *once* (Mark 5:9). Again, this had to do with one man's problem, not that of a whole province or territory. Moreover, the apostles never told young ministers such as Timothy or Titus to inquire about demons' names.

Please don't misunderstand: I fully believe that the devil invades people's lives today and has to be confronted. I have had to confront him a number of times in my ministry. One Tuesday night two members of the church brought a teenager to the prayer meeting who, they said, was on drugs and needed to be delivered. That's all they told me. I didn't think too much about it; this kind of thing happens often. (Our wonderful members don't know better than to bring the unconverted to a prayer meeting!)

About a half hour into the meeting, after we had been worshiping for a while, I said, "There's a girl here who's been brought by some members, and they'd like her to be prayed for; she's hooked on drugs."

These members began walking toward the front with a short Hispanic girl. She seemed in a daze—the effect of drugs, I assumed. Her name was Diana.

I was standing, as I usually do on Tuesday nights, on the ground level with the people, at the head of the center aisle. All of a sudden, I began to tense up; alarm bells seemed to be going off in my spirit signifying that something was wrong—something was about to happen.

I noticed off to my right a visiting evangelist I knew. I said to her, "Amy, it's good to see you here tonight. Would you come help me pray for this young lady?" As she moved out of her seat, the Holy Spirit came upon her, and she sensed the same anticipation. We were suddenly both on "red alert" for some unknown reason.

One of the associate pastors joined us, and we laid hands on Diana and began to pray. "O Jesus, help us," I said quietly.

Like a shot, the mention of Jesus' name brought an explosion of rage and screaming. The five-foot-one-inch girl lunged for my throat, throwing back the two friends who had guided her up the aisle. Before I knew what was happening,

I had been body-slammed against the front edge of the platform. Diana ripped the collar right off my white shirt as if it were a piece of tissue. A hideous voice from deep inside her began to scream, "You'll never have her! She's ours! Get away from her!" The language then turned obscene.

The five-foot-one-inch girl lunged for my throat. Before I knew what was happening, I had been body-slammed backward against the platform. ✿

Some in the congregation stood and began to pray aloud. Others gasped. Some covered their eyes. Meanwhile, several deacons jumped up and tried to pull her off of me. Despite her size, she fought all of us with tremendous strength.

We finally managed to subdue her. Amy, the evangelist, began to pray fervently. I leaned over the girl to address the spirits: "Shut up! In the name of Jesus, come out of her!" I demanded.

Diana's eyes rolled back in her head, and twice she spit directly into my face, no more than a foot away. The church kept earnestly calling out to God for his help. Clearly, we were not battling some imaginary "spirit of anger" or whatever. This was a classic case of demon possession.

Within a few minutes, the girl was set totally free. She stopped cursing; her body relaxed. We relaxed our grip on her, and she gently stood up to raise her hands and begin praising the Lord. Soon she was singing, with the rest of us, "Oh, the blood of Jesus! It washes white as snow," as tears streamed down her cheeks, ruining her makeup.

Diana has been serving the Lord for ten years now in the Brooklyn Tabernacle. Recently she married a young man, and both of them gave strong testimonies of their faith in front of mostly unbelieving relatives. She is a wonderful Christian today who loves the Lord and wants to serve him alone.

Diana has allowed me to tell her story to make the point that I believe in confronting satanic activity. Was her experience unique or weird? Not by New Testament standards. This was just "mere Christianity," the kind of thing Jesus and the apostles did on a regular basis.

But we should not expect to discover new shortcuts in the spiritual realm. Have we forgotten that when Jesus sent out his twelve disciples, he specifically "gave them authority to drive out evil spirits" ... yet he also told them that some towns would not welcome them. "They will hand you over to the local councils and flog you in their synagogues" (Matt. 10:1, 17). If the twelve, with one sweep of the hand, could have bound the opposing spirit in that city, wouldn't Jesus have explained this? It would have spared Christians a lot of conflict.

Instead, Jesus addressed the various churches in the book of Revelation with somber warnings about the opposition they were facing:

To Smyrna: "I tell you, the devil will put some of you in prison to test you, and you will suffer persecution for ten days. Be faithful, even to the point of death" (Rev. 2:10). Christ warns that they are in a hostile environment and there are no quick fixes.

To Pergamum: "I know where you live—where Satan has his throne." The next sentence does not read: *Kick him out! Bind him!* No. Jesus calmly continues, "Yet you remain true to my name. You did not renounce your faith in me, even in the days of Antipas, my faithful witness, who was put to death in your city—where Satan lives" (Rev. 2:13).

The all-knowing King of kings and Lord of lords, who holds the keys of death and hell, tells the Christians to battle through. In both these letters Jesus describes what Satan was permitted to do, within the limits of some sovereign plan of God that we don't fully comprehend. Nevertheless, the believers are to press ahead with old-fashioned spiritual endurance.

The trouble with today's man-made novelties is that they simply don't produce the impressive results that are often advertised. They do not, so far as I know, result in masses of people being converted, being baptized in water, or forming strong, prayerful churches. Where is the city anywhere in the world that has been "taken for God," as the rhetoric often claims? Wouldn't it be wiser, as Paul said, to "not boast beyond proper limits" (2 Cor. 10:13) but rather let the Spirit produce results that speak for themselves?

Just as some say the powers of evil are attached to certain locales, others are proclaiming certain centers of God's "new anointing." Certain cities are said to be chosen for a unique out-pouring of the Holy Spirit. Where do we find this in Scripture?

It is totally unbiblical to insinuate that people must travel to a particular church anywhere to receive what God has for them. There is no special anointing from the Brooklyn Tabernacle or any other church that can be passed on by the laying on of hands. Nowhere in the book of Acts do people travel to Jerusalem or any other city to be "where the action is."

All we find in the New Testament is the admonition to "come near to God and he will come near to you" (James 4:8). The responsibility lies with us. If enough people in New York City or San Francisco call out to God with all their hearts, those cities can become world-famous for revival. God is no respecter of geography.

We are too easily distracted from the call to simply wait on the Lord. We get pulled away from the simplicity of the gospel. In Acts 4, the apostles only wanted to preach the Word. It sounds too minimal to modern ears, doesn't it—

isn't there something more, something greater, something newer?

In the face of a world ignoring Christ's offer of salvation, we can either humble ourselves before God and return to his basics ... or we can go on dancing with ourselves. The potential to see local churches explode with the life of God rests in the balance.

NO HOCUS-POCUS

THERE IS NO BETTER example of God's moving mightily in a city than the account told in Acts 11:20–21: "... men from Cyprus and Cyrene, went to Antioch and began to speak to Greeks ... telling them the good news about the Lord Jesus. The Lord's hand was with them, and a great number of people believed and turned to the Lord."

Such a harvest occurred that Barnabas was dispatched from Jerusalem to check things out. "When he arrived and saw the evidence of the grace of God, he was glad.... And a great number of people were brought to the Lord" (vv. 23–24).

Who were these men who launched such a mighty church that it eventually surpassed the mother church in Jerusalem? We don't know their names. We don't know their methodology. We don't know whether they were premillennial or postmillennial or amillennial. But we do know a couple of things: They spread "the good news about the Lord Jesus," and "the Lord's hand was with them" (vv. 20–21).

This turned out to be the first truly multicultural church, with multicultural leaders, according to Acts 13:1—Simon the Black, some Jewish leaders, some Greeks, Manaen the boyhood friend of Herod (which would have made him suspect to everyone!), and others. Yet they worked together in a powerful model of cross-cultural unity.

The Jewish-Gentile hatred of the first century was even greater than our racial strife today. God met this problem head-on, for he was building his church his way.

Racial feelings in New York City are worse now than they were ten years ago. A harsh spirit prevails in many churches. We desperately need the love of God to override these tensions, as it did in Antioch long ago.

No novel teaching is going to turn the trick. There are no trendy shortcuts, no hocus-pocus mantras that can defeat Satan.

One man told me, "You know, you ought to think about getting a topographical map of Brooklyn so you could figure out the highest point in the borough. Then you could go there and pray against the territorial spirits."

I wanted to say, "Brother, that is nothing but Old Testament sorcery. The idolaters of Elijah's time were into 'high places,' remember?" They somehow thought they could get a better angle on the demons, I guess. I don't care if I led my whole congregation over to the one-hundred-and-first-floor observation deck of the World Trade Center towers—we would get a wonderful view of Brooklyn, but we wouldn't impress God. Or the devil, for that matter.

Others are saying, "The key to releasing God's power is to *sing* through the streets of your city. Put on a march, make banners, and declare God's sovereignty in a big parade." While Christians may enjoy such an outing, does it really make a measurable difference in a community?

Still others say, "Rebuke the devil, face the north, and stamp your feet when you do it. That will bring victory."

On vacation, Carol and I watched a Sunday morning church service on television in which the pastor was emphasizing spiritual warfare. He was in the pulpit *dressed in military fatigues!* This was supposed to scare the devil, I guess. We weren't sure whether to laugh or cry.

Can someone show me where the New Testament attaches any promise to the movement of our bodies or how we clothe them? When bizarre physical manifestations become the official sign of a supposed new awakening, we have abandoned our biblical roots. Only trouble lies ahead.

Let's forget the novelties. If we prevail in prayer, God will do what only he can do. How he does things, when he does them, and in what manner are up to him. The name of Jesus, the power of his blood, and the prayer of faith have not lost their power over the centuries.

When Charles Finney preached in Rochester, New York, in the 1820s, more than 100,000 people came to Christ within a year. "The whole community was stirred," according to one eyewitness. "Grog [liquor] shops were closed; the Sabbath was honored; the sanctuaries were thronged with happy worshipers.... Even the courts and the prisons bore witness to [the] blessed effects. There was a wonderful falling off in crime. The courts had little to do, and the jail was nearly empty for years afterward."[1]

I can assure you that Finney didn't "bind the spirit of alcohol" or anything else; he just did God's work in God's way, and a whole city was affected.

During the Welsh revival around 1904, according to historian J. Edwin Orr, a police sergeant told the local newspaper, "There are seventeen churches in our town, and we have quartets of policemen ready to provide music to any church that wants it." That was because the cops had little else to do with their time. Even the criminals were apparently in church, where a young coal miner named Evan Roberts led most of the meetings by praying rather than preaching.

When G. Campbell Morgan and other distinguished churchmen came from London to observe the revival, they could not get into the building; they were reduced to peering over other people's heads out in the vestibule. Did they hear Roberts calling for a march to the high places of the Welsh mountains? In fact, the opposite: Roberts was often overheard to pray, "Lower, Lord—take us lower." He would fall on his knees and begin to groan out his intercession for Wales, following the biblical pattern of humbling oneself in prayer (see James 4:9–10 and 1 Peter 5:6).

There was also a wave of bankruptcies in Wales during those years—mostly taverns.

THE BIBLE IS ENOUGH

AS A MINISTER I firmly believe that I am not allowed to preach what is not in the Bible. It is an exciting enough book as it stands. It is not something dull that we need to spice up. If we do and teach all that Jesus did and taught—and no more—we will have plenty of thrills. Otherwise, let us be silent where the Bible is silent.

> As a minister I firmly believe that I am not allowed to preach what is not in the Bible. It is an exciting enough book as it stands. ❧

The apostle Paul put it plainly in his letter to the church at Corinth, which had gotten itself into several messes. He was trying to move the people back on track, so he urged them to "learn from us the meaning of the saying, 'Do not go beyond what is written'" (1 Cor. 4:6). Apparently Paul thought that a scriptural foundation was essential, and beyond that lay little more than trouble.

Meanwhile, he told the Galatians, "Even if we or an angel from heaven should preach a gospel other than the one we preached to you, let him be eternally condemned!" (Gal. 1:8).

I love what William J. Seymour wrote—the one-eyed, marginally educated African-American elder at the Azusa Street Mission in Los Angeles, where the modern Pentecostal movement took shape in 1906. "We are measuring everything by the Word," he wrote in the September 1907 issue of *Apostolic Faith* magazine. "Every experience must measure up with the Bible. Some say that is going too far [in other words, being too strict!], but if we have lived too close to the Word, we will settle that with the Lord when we meet Him in the air."

> **No one has the right to adjust the gospel or
> revise God's plan for his church.** ❦

No one has the right to adjust the gospel or revise God's plan for his church. Those precious things are not yours or mine; they are God's. We need to stop fussing with them. We need to submit to the heavenly design laid down long ago.

DEEPER, NOT WIDER

THE THINGS OF GOD have a circumference. They are preserved in a written body of truth. It is like a well—and no one has ever fathomed the depth of God's truth.

To go into the power of the gospel, or of prayer, or the Holy Spirit, or divine love is to plunge ever deeper and deeper into God's well. Every man or woman used by God has gone *down* into this vast reservoir.

The tendency today, however, is merely to splash around in truth for a while ... and then jump *outside* the well to the surrounding soil. "Look at this—God is doing a new thing!" people proclaim. In six months or so, of course, the novelty wears off, and they jump again to a new patch of grass. They spend their whole lives hopscotching from one side of God's well to another, never really probing the depth of the living waters inside.

Inside the well there is no cause for leaving or jumping out. Who will ever fathom the fullness of the love of God? Who will ever exhaust the richness of his mercy to fallen human beings? Who will ever understand the real power of prayer?

Especially since the 1960s, fads have come and gone in the North American church, only to be replaced by newer fads. Leonard Ravenhill, the revival-minded preacher and author from Britain, told me shortly before he died, "People say the church today is 'growing and expanding.' Yes, it's ten miles wide now—and about a quarter-inch deep."

Deliverance from the dark powers has especially captured our fantasies. While Jesus and the apostles did indeed cast out demons from the unsaved, nowhere do we see this being done for the benefit of Christians. Nowhere do we find Paul saying, "You know, you Corinthians have a real mess there. You need to get the elders of the church together, have them go into earnest prayer, and then anoint the church members with oil to cast out the 'spirit of gossip' in your church. The folks who are overweight need to have the 'demon of fat' cast out of them. The immoral brother who's living with his stepmother needs to be delivered from the 'spirit of lust.' . . ."

Paul had a much more mundane explanation for these problems: They were simply "works of the flesh." He called for repentance, for dying daily to self—not flamboyant exorcism.

Just as our culture in general is taken up with a victim mentality, where everything is somebody else's fault, to be relieved by psychotherapy, government handouts, or litigation, so in the church people are saying, "It's the devil's fault. Don't blame me." No wonder there is little brokenness of spirit among us. Why pray and confess if your main problem is oppression (or possession) by an evil spirit that someone else needs to get off your back? Few Christians or sermons use the word "sin" anymore. Few sense the need to repent of their own wrongdoing. Rather, they look to the outside for a scapegoat.

When you work in the inner city, as I do, the victim mentality can be very strong. "I'm black, or brown, so it's hard for me to get anywhere in life.... I was molested as a child by my uncle, and I'm still dealing with the pain of that...."

I often reply, "Yes, those things are real—but God is greater. None of us can afford to blame the past indefinitely. My father, in fact, was an alcoholic for twenty-one years, to the point that he lost his career at Westinghouse. His weekend binges eventually stretched to entire weeks, then a full month. When he was drinking, he would call me every four-letter word I'd ever heard, and some I hadn't.... He even missed my wedding.

"So I should accomplish absolutely nothing in life, right?

"Not at all. I am still responsible. I have no license from God to lie down and vegetate. God can still hold me and put me to work in his service."

I usually go on to point out a wonderful detail in the life of Joseph, the young man whose brothers sold him into Egyptian slavery. After being framed by Potiphar's wife, thrown into prison, and forgotten ... when he finally married and had a son, he named him Manasseh, which means "to forget." He said, "It is because God has made me forget all my trouble and all my father's household" (Gen. 41:51). God is more powerful than anybody's past, no matter how wretched. He can make us forget—not by erasing the memory but by taking the sting and paralyzing effect out of it.

I am thankful that my father's life has been redeemed in recent times. He has been sober for more than thirteen years. Today he loves the Lord with all his heart, as does my mother. They are both faithful members and a tremendous support to the Brooklyn Tabernacle.

ALL NEEDS ALREADY SUPPLIED

IF WE VENTURE INTO a gymnasium these days, we are likely to run into fellows who look like superstars in expensive Adidas sneakers, color-coordinated knee bands and all the rest. The only trouble is, they can't get the ball into the hoop. They have all the latest gear, but they still can't play.

We as God's people have all the equipment we need. It has been around for two thousand years. He has given us everything necessary to put points on the scoreboard and win victories in his name. So let us move forward with full confidence in what we have received.

Nothing about God will change. Tomorrow he will be no more anxious to help our lives, our families, and our churches then than he is right now. If we simply avail ourselves of his promises, we will see him do things we could never ask or think, just as he did in the New Testament. It is time to press on.

EIGHT

The Lure of Marketing

Have you noticed that whenever you ask a fellow Christian these days about his or her church, the subject invariably goes to *attendance?*

Question: "Tell me about your church. How is the Lord's work coming along there?"

Answer: "Well, we have about three hundred on Sunday, I'd say."

When I ask fellow pastors the same question, I get the same answer—plus two others: "Membership is at five-fifty, we've just finished a new education wing, and our gross income this year will top out at about four hundred thousand."

Attendance, buildings, and cash. A-B-C: The new holy trinity.

HOW BIG WAS ANTIOCH?

Such a thing would never have happened in Peter and Paul's day. For one thing, they had no buildings to call their own. They met in people's homes, in public courtyards, sometimes even in caves. As for budget, they seemed to have dispensed most of their funds in helping the poor.

Headcounts hardly appear after the Day of Pentecost. We notice a couple of large numbers in Acts 2:41 and 4:4. Later on, Acts 19:7 says "about twelve men" in Ephesus were filled with the Holy Spirit under Paul's ministry. Beyond that, we know nothing. In 1 Corinthians 1:14–16, Paul can't even remember whom he baptized, let alone the total count.

How large was the attendance in the Antioch church? Berea? Philippi? Rome? We have no idea.

How large was the congregation at Philadelphia, one of the seven churches addressed in the book of Revelation? Apparently, not very big. The Lord says, "I know that you have little strength." Yet he proceeds to give them a glowing review (Rev. 3:7–13).

> **No church, including the one I pastor, should be measured by its attendance.** ❧

By contrast, how large was the congregation at Laodicea? One can get a hint from the fact that the church was "rich and in need of nothing." For all we know, it may have drawn 7,000 on a Sunday. Their bills were certainly paid—yet they received a scathing spiritual rebuke.

Nowhere in the epistles do we find Paul saying, "I hear your attendance was down last quarter—what's the problem? What are you going to do about it?"

This leads me to say that no church, including the one I pastor, should be measured by its attendance. Although I am thankful for the crowds of people who come to the Brooklyn Tabernacle every week, that is not the sign of God's grace.

BEYOND POPULARITY

THEN WHAT KIND OF spiritual things *do* matter in a book-of-Acts church? The apostles' prayer in Acts 4 provides our next benchmark: "Enable your servants to speak your word *with great boldness*" (v. 29). What the disciples wanted was not numbers but an essential quality that would keep them *being* the church God intended.

Boldness can only be imparted by the Holy Spirit. There is no such thing as "taught boldness." You cannot get it through a seminar. Second Timothy 1:7 says, "For God did not give us a spirit of timidity, but a spirit of power, of love and of self-discipline."

New Testament preachers were boldly confrontational, trusting that the Holy Spirit would produce the conviction necessary for conversion. They were not afraid.

Listen to Peter on the Day of Pentecost: "You, with the help of wicked men, put him to death by nailing him to the cross" (Acts 2:23). This was the *last* thing the crowd wanted to hear. If David Letterman had a Top Ten list of things *not* to say to a Jewish audience, number one would be "Guess what—with your own hands you just killed the Messiah, the one Israel has been expecting for centuries."

But Peter's boldness did not drive the people away. Instead, it stabbed their consciences. By the end of the day a huge group had repented of their sin and been converted.

In the next chapter, Peter was just as straightforward with the crowd that gathered after the healing of the cripple: "You disowned the Holy and Righteous One and asked that a murderer be released to you. You killed the author of life.... Repent, then, and turn to God, so that your sins may be wiped out, that times of refreshing may come from the Lord" (Acts 3:14–15, 19).

When Paul preached in Ephesus some years later, his confrontation with the pagan idolatry was so direct that a riot broke out. "They were furious and began shouting: 'Great is Artemis of the Ephesians!' Soon the whole city was in an uproar" (Acts 19:28–29). This doesn't sound very market-sensitive or user-friendly to me.

A strong church was established nonetheless. And when Paul bade them farewell, he could say, "I have not hesitated to proclaim to you the whole will of God.... Remember that for three years I never stopped warning each of you night and day with tears" (Acts 20:27, 31). Notice: "the *whole* will of God ... I never stopped *warning* you." This was at the heart of apostolic ministry.

The apostles realized that without a bold, aggressive attitude in proclaiming God's Word, they would not build the church Jesus intended. Any church in any city of the world must come to the same conclusion.

The apostles weren't trying to finesse people. Their communication was not supposed to be "cool" or soothing. They aimed for a piercing of the heart, for conviction of sin. They had not the faintest intention of asking, "What do people want to hear? How can we draw more people to church on Sunday?" That was the last thing in their minds. Such an approach would have been foreign to the whole New Testament.

> **The apostles weren't trying to finesse people. They had not the faintest intention of asking, "What do people want to hear? How can we draw more people to church on Sunday?"** ❧

Instead of trying to bring men and women to Christ in the biblical way, we are consumed with the unbiblical concept of "church growth." The Bible does not say we should aim at numbers but rather urges us faithfully to proclaim God's message in the boldness of the Holy Spirit. This will build God's church God's way.

Unfortunately, some churches now continually monitor how pleased people are with the services and ask what else they would like. One denominational specialist told a reporter, "We need to learn how to surf with changes."[1]

We have no permission whatsoever to adjust the message of the gospel. Whether it seems popular or not, whether it is "hip" to the times, we must faithfully and boldly proclaim that sin is real but Jesus forgives those who confess.

God nowhere asks anyone to have a large church. He only calls us to do his work, proclaiming his Word to people he loves under the anointing and power of the Holy Spirit to produce results that only he can bring about. The glory then goes to him alone—not to any denomination, local church, local pastor, or church-growth consultant. That is God's only plan, and anything else is a deviation from the teaching of the New Testament.

God told Ezekiel that if wicked people needed a warning and he failed to deliver it, their blood would be on the prophet's hands. The same holds true today for ministers of the Word.

Dwight L. Moody was haunted all his life by an occasion when he felt he got too clever in presenting the gospel. Six years before he died he recounted what had happened back in Chicago in the fall of 1871:

> I intended to devote six nights to Christ's life. I had spent four Sunday nights on the subject and had followed him from the manger along through his life to his arrest and trial, and on the fifth Sunday night, October 8, I was preaching to the largest congregation I had ever had in Chicago, quite elated with my success. My text was "What shall I do then with Jesus which is called the Christ?" That night I made one of the biggest mistakes of my life. After preaching ... with all the power that God had given me, urging Christ upon the people, I closed the sermon and said, "I wish you

would take this text home with you and turn it over in your minds during the week, and next Sunday we will come to Calvary and the cross, and we will decide what we will do with Jesus of Nazareth."

Just at that moment, a fire bell rang nearby. Moody quickly dismissed the meeting and sent the people out of the building. It was the beginning of the Great Chicago Fire, which over the next 27 hours left 300 dead, 90,000 homeless, and a great city in ashes. Obviously, Moody never got to finish his sermon series.

He continued:

> I have never seen that congregation since. I have hard work to keep back the tears today.... Twenty-two years have passed away ... and I will never meet those people again until I meet them in another world. But I want to tell you one lesson I learned that night, which I have never forgotten, and that is, when I preach to press Christ upon the people then and there, I try to bring them to a decision on the spot. I would rather have [my] right hand cut off than give an audience a week to decide what to do with Jesus.

No wonder the apostle James wrote, "Why, you do not even know what will happen tomorrow. What is your life? You are a mist that appears for a little while and then vanishes" (4:14). The gospel is too important to be left to tomorrow, or next week, or when the crowd seems friendlier.

Did John Wesley, preaching to hardened miners in the open fields of England in the 1700s, ever say to himself, *I had better not tell them they're sinners; they might leave?*

Today we have an anti-authority spirit in America that says, "Nobody can tell me I need to change. Don't you dare."

Both in the pulpit and in pastoral counseling we have too often given in to this mentality and are afraid to speak the truth about sin. We keep appealing to Paul's line about becoming "all things to all men" (1 Cor. 9:22), not noticing that in the very next paragraph he says, "Run in such a way as to get the prize" (v. 24). Adapting our style to get a hearing is one thing, but the message can never change without leaving us empty-handed before the Lord.

> **Today, we have an anti-authority spirit in America that says, "Nobody can tell me I need to change. Don't you dare."** ❧

Do we still believe the truth of Proverbs 28:23, where it says, "He who rebukes a man will in the end gain more favor than he who has a flattering tongue"?

Jesus was confrontational. When Peter told him to avoid the cross, Jesus didn't reply, "You know, Peter, I'm really trying to understand where you're coming from. I appreciate how you care about me and don't want me to get hurt." Rather, he said to his number-one disciple, "Get behind me, Satan! You are a stumbling block to me; you do not have in mind the things of God, but the things of men" (Matt. 16:23).

What do *we* have in mind?

GETTING TO THE POINT

I HAVE FOUND THAT about 90 percent of the time, the problems people describe to me are not their real problems. Therefore the challenge in all preaching and counseling is to get to the bottom-line spiritual issue. A husband says, "She doesn't understand me." It is easy to reply, "Yes, that's too bad. I feel sorry for you." But what may be really going on is that he's acting like a brute.

Graciously but firmly, we have to speak the truth in love.

An attractive young couple, whom I will call Michelle and Steve, came forward for prayer at the end of a Sunday service. Both were nicely dressed—he in an expensive suit and $60 silk tie, she in a fashionable dress. I could tell by the moisture in her eyes that something had touched her during the service. By contrast, he seemed to hold back just a step, not looking me in the eye.

"Would you please pray for us?" she asked.

"Certainly," I said. "What would you like me to pray about?"

"That God will bless our relationship," she replied.

That line can mean anything, especially in New York City. I felt prompted to ask a few more questions.

"Uh, before I pray, help me with a little background, if you will. How long have you known each other?"

"A couple of years."

The next question wasn't exactly polite, but I felt the Spirit nudging me. So, without the slightest change in my voice level or inflection, I said, "Are you living together?"

The shock was instantaneous. Her eyelashes blinked; his head snapped up. We stood there frozen for a second, staring at each other. Finally she answered, "Well, uh … yes, we are."

I nodded, then said, "Okay, that puts me in sort of a bind. You want me to ask God to bless something that he has already expressed his opinion about. He's already made it clear in the Bible that living together outside of marriage is wrong. So it looks to me like I'd be wasting everybody's time to ask his help in this situation, wouldn't I?"

They just stared at me. I pressed on.

"I tell you what—let's get on track with God's plan. Steve, how about you finding another place to live—right now? You say you want God's best for your relationship. Okay, this is step number one. This will open the door for many other good things."

I could tell Steve wasn't thrilled with the idea.

"Do you have family or friends in the city where you could stay tonight?"

No, he couldn't think of anyone.

"Listen, we'll get you a place to stay," I said. "If God is real and you truly want his help in your life, then go his way. Otherwise, do whatever you like! Of course, it will destroy you in the end; you can't change God's consequences any more than you can change the law of gravity."

He mumbled another excuse. I called one of the lay helpers over and requested that Steve be provided with a bed for the night.

Steve and Michelle still weren't sure. "How about if we stay where we are but just don't sleep together? That would be all right, wouldn't it?"

I replied, "If you both profess to be Christians, you have to avoid the obvious physical temptation. Besides, when you walk out of your apartment in the morning, what would a neighbor logically assume? Do this thing right, all the way, okay?"

They finally agreed to the plan.

Some couples in the same situation, I must tell you, have not agreed. They have said things like "Well, we'll get back to you about that" and walked out. But at least I could rest at night knowing I had told them the truth before God.

I have also received follow-up letters from women saying, "You know, I didn't like what you said to my boyfriend and me that day. You showed us what we needed to hear from the Bible, but we didn't want to accept it. Anyway, I thought

I should let you know that in time, he left me, just as you said. I was a piece of meat, nothing more. Now I'm alone again, and I wish I would have listened."

Steve and Michelle's situation turned out better. He immediately found another place to live. We kept working with them and gave them counseling. God opened their eyes to spiritual realities. Then something wonderful happened. On a Tuesday night, as the prayer meeting was drawing to a close, I said, "Before you all leave, I have a surprise for you tonight. Everybody stand, please."

The congregation rose . . . and the organist began the stately octaves of Lohengrin's "Wedding March." The rear doors opened and the smiling bride, in a simple street-length dress and holding flowers, moved forward. The people broke into wild applause. Steve, who had been sitting near me on the front row all evening, stood for the ceremony. In front of 1,500 witnesses, they were united in Christ.

Several times during the proceedings, their quiet weeping for joy became so loud it could be heard through my microphone. They managed to say their vows nevertheless. After the recessional I said to the audience, "You know, that couple just recently came to the Lord." I didn't go into the unseemly details of their past, but most people could figure it out. They knew full well the grace and power of God to make crooked things straight.

This kind of thing has happened a number of times on Tuesday nights over the years. It is always a wonderful celebration.

Pleasing Whom?

The staff of the Brooklyn Tabernacle have taken a bold stand even in complicated cases, as when the couple who are living together have children. To ask the man to move out temporarily but keep on paying the bills is tough. Those who are earnest about repenting, however, have followed through just that way.

I often say to cohabiting couples, "You're probably wondering, *What's this preacher's angle? What is he trying to prove?* I have no angle other than to please God. As you can see, the church building is already full; we're not desperate for new members or your contributions in the offering. But we *are* desperate to please God and not be ashamed when we stand before him someday."

The apostle Paul expressed his conviction this way in 1 Thessalonians 2:4. "We are not trying to please men but God, who tests our hearts." God didn't ask Carol and me to build a big church. He told us to preach the gospel and love people in his name. Some listeners reject the truth while others open up. It has been this way throughout history, but the results are always more dynamic and glorious when we do things God's way.

> God didn't ask Carol and me to build a big church. He told us to preach the gospel and love people in his name. ❧

Just as the Israelites were warned not to mingle with the Canaanite gods called Baal or Asherah, we must beware a god in our time called Success. Bigger is not better if it comes at the expense of disowning the truth or grieving the Holy Spirit.

Imagine a basketball court with hoops five feet off the ground. The free-throw line is three feet away. I've just made 884 free throws in a row.

My wife walks out to watch and says, "What are you doing?"

"I'm playing basketball. See, here's the ball, and there's the hoop on a backboard. The lines are all marked and everything."

Carol would say, "No, the hoop is supposed to be ten feet high, and the line is supposed to be fifteen feet away. *That* is basketball. What you're doing is nothing more than a charade."

We have a lot of markings that look like Christianity these days, but we have drastically revised the parameters. People have lowered the standards in a vain attempt to make churches look more successful than they really are. The sermons have to be uniformly positive, and the services can't go longer than 60 minutes. Even then, church is inconvenient for some, especially during football season. Showing up at church is such a burden that soon people will be faxing in their worship!

> **Showing up at church is such a burden that soon people will be faxing in their worship!** ❦

One minister told me recently that two families left for another church because his parking attendants didn't direct cars out of the lot fast enough. What would these people have done the night in Troas when Paul preached until midnight? (See Acts 20:7.)

Can you imagine someone handing Peter a microphone on Sunday morning and whispering, "Okay, now, you've got twenty minutes. We have to get the people out of here promptly because the chariot races start at one o'clock"?

The truth is that "user-friendly" can be a cover-up word for carnality. The same people who want sixty-minute worship services rent two-hour videos and watch NBA and NFL games that run even longer. The issue is not length, but appetite. Why the misplaced desire?

Seriously, what will our children and grandchildren grow up experiencing in church? Extended times of waiting on the Lord will be totally foreign to their experience. There will be no memory bank of seeing people reach out to God. All they will recall are professionally polished, closely timed productions.

One of our soloists recently went to sing in a church and was told in advance, "We want to ask you not to sing any song that mentions the blood of Christ. People feel uncomfortable with that, and our goal here is to be user-friendly."

If people really don't appreciate the word *blood* in the sense of sacrifice, why are we so open to Fourth of July speakers referring to the sacrifice of the brave men and women who fought to defend America? Should we avoid mentioning the blood that was shed for political liberty? If not, how much more should we honor the blood of the Lamb of God, no matter what others think?

The message of the cross will always be foolishness to some, a stumbling block to others. But if our attention is on the market reaction, we move away from the power of the gospel. This fearfulness to talk about the blood of Christ is an overreaction. Worse than that, it borders on heresy, distorting and deflating the power of the Good News.

What has become of standing unashamed for the gospel of Christ? No one is smarter than God. When he says to do his work in his way, we can be assured that he will produce his results for his glory. We don't need to get "creative" on him. God knows exactly what we need to do and expects us to trust and obey him in childlike simplicity.

God does not ask us to be clever in appealing to those who want a worldly type of wisdom. It is not by might, not by power, not by computers, not by cleverness, but by my Spirit, says the Lord (see Zech. 4:6).

These days we are so programmed that God couldn't break in if he wanted to. During times of worship in many churches, the schedule of songs and hymns is so rigid that nothing, not even God's Spirit, can interrupt. The worship leaders have the musical key changes memorized and everything. If God could lead the Israelites for 40 years in the wilderness, can't he lead us through one meeting, one praise-and-worship time, without a lineup? A basic sign of revival is that the wind is allowed to blow where it will.

We don't need technicians and church programmers; *we need God.* He is not looking for smart people, because he's the smart one. All he wants are people simple enough to trust him.

According to 1 Corinthians 14, if meetings are governed by the Holy Spirit, the result for the visitor will be that "the secrets of his heart will be laid bare. So he will fall down and worship God, exclaiming, 'God is really among you!'" (v. 25). This should be our goal. When a visitor comes in, there should be such a mixture of God's truth and God's presence that the person's heart is x-rayed, the futility of his life is exposed, and he crumbles in repentance.

Are we longing for this? Are we praying for this? Are today's church leaders aiming for this? Are church members encouraging their pastors to act on the Lord's prompting no matter the cost?

Alexander Whyte, after observing the 1859 awakening in Scotland, made this marvelous statement: "In revival, the congregation does the preaching." What he meant was that, beyond the presence of preachers, musicians, and other ministries, what speaks to the heart is that God is dwelling in close communion with his people.

THE REAL TEST

AT A MUSIC CONFERENCE where I spoke, a gentleman approached me with tears in his eyes. "We've just gotten a new pastor," he said. "And his instructions to me, as the minister of music, are: 'Please discontinue "church music." I want you to look for choral music from Broadway, from the pop scene, for the Sunday meetings.'

"What am I going to do? I want to relate to people the same as he does—but does that mean I can't honor the Lord's name in our music, as I always have?"

I told him he had no choice but to go back to his pastor and open his heart. They needed to have a long talk.

There will come a day, Paul says, when all our "work will be shown for what it is, because the Day will bring it to light. It will be revealed with fire, and the fire will test the quality of each man's work" (1 Cor. 3:13). The gold, silver, and precious stones will endure while the wood, hay, and straw will go up in smoke.

Paul doesn't say that the *quantity* will be tested. He says nothing about attendance totals. Everything will focus on *quality*.

Warren Wiersbe made an interesting observation about this passage to the Brooklyn Tabernacle staff. "What's the difference between these materials, besides the obvious—that one group is fireproof while the other isn't?

"I think it's significant that wood, hay, and straw are abundant ... right outside your door, or only a few miles away at most. Any forest, any farmer's field has an abundance of these.

"But if you want gold, silver, and costly stones, you have to *dig* for them. You have to pursue with great effort. They're not just lying around everywhere. You have to go deep into the earth."

To me, these words are profound. Spiritual "construction" that uses wood, hay, and straw comes easy—little work, little seeking, no travail, no birthing. You just slap it up and it will look adequate—for a while. But if you want to build something that will endure on Judgment Day, the work is much more costly.

On that day it won't matter what your fellow Christians thought of you. It won't matter what the marketing experts advised. You and I will stand before the One whose eyes are "like fire." We won't soften him up by telling him how brilliant our strategy was. We will face his searing gaze.

He will only ask whether we were boldly faithful to his Word.

NINE

The Lure of Doctrine Without Power

I HAVE NOT MEANT to portray New York City as totally god-less and pagan, because in fact, Brooklyn has historically been known as "the borough of churches." We have countless buildings that once housed active, vibrant congregations. Unfortunately, they are almost empty today. As the neighborhoods "changed," as drugs became more prevalent, the momentum faded.

Many parishioners died or moved into the suburbs but generously left large endowments. Today these churches may have pitifully few people in the pews on Sunday but they can still pay a pastor's full-time salary and keep the enterprise going. One of the most famous is a downtown church we used to rent for special outreach events. The sanctuary, which seats 1,400, was packed in the 1930s and 1940s, but it has not been used for regular Sunday worship since the 1960s. The congregation currently meets in the basement.

Inner cities have thus become a forgotten mission field. Church buildings are empty in places where they should be crowded. Sin is abounding—but contrary to Romans 5, grace is *not* abounding more.

Is this because the pulpits are not declaring truth?

In some cases, yes—but in many cases, no. That may surprise you if you have assumed that the decline is always due to theological liberalism or false doctrine. But many groups who own these silent sanctuaries are as orthodox as a church could be. If you quizzed them about the divinity of Christ, the Virgin Birth, or their adherence to the Apostles' Creed, they would pass with flying colors.

So what is missing?

BEYOND HEAD KNOWLEDGE

THE ABSENT ELEMENT IS what is expressed in the final sentence of the prayer recorded in Acts 4: "Stretch out your hand to heal and perform miraculous signs and wonders" (v. 30). What gains unbelievers' attention and stirs the heart is seeing the gospel expressed in power.

It takes more than academic rigor to win the world for Christ. Correct doctrine alone isn't enough. Proclamation and teaching aren't enough. God must be invited to "confirm the word with signs following" (see Heb. 2:4). In other words, the gospel must be preached *with* the involvement of the Holy Spirit sent down from heaven.

> It takes more than academic rigor to win the world for Christ. Correct doctrine alone won't do it. ❦

The apostles prayed for God to do supernatural things. They wanted people to know their belief was more than positional or theoretical. There was *power* in this faith. "O God, stretch out your hand—work with us in this." They wanted a faith that was obviously alive, a faith based not just on the cross but also on the empty tomb. The cross, as poignant as it is, is understandable from a human perspective: an innocent man was murdered by crooked politicians and religious leaders. But the empty tomb—what can you say? Only a supernatural God could accomplish that.

In too many churches today, people don't see manifestations of God's power in answer to fervent praying. Instead, they hear arguments about theological issues that few people care about. On Christian radio and television we are often merely talking to ourselves.

What we are dealing with today is an Old Testament "vow religion" comprised of endless repetitions and commands to do all the right things. Modern preachers, like Moses, come down from the mount calling for commitment. Everyone says yes but then promptly breaks the vow within two days. There is little dependence on God's power to make an ongoing difference. There is little calling upon God to revolutionize us in a supernatural way.

Jesus is saying today, as he said to the church at Sardis, "You have a reputation of being alive, but you are dead. Wake up! Strengthen what remains and is about to die, for I have not found your deeds complete in the sight of my God.... But if you do not wake up, I will come like a thief.... He who has an ear, let him hear what the Spirit says to the churches" (Rev. 3:1–3, 6).

Isn't it remarkable that only two of the seven churches of Revelation (Pergamum and Thyatira) were scolded for false doctrine? Far more common was a lack of spiritual vitality, of fervency, of closeness to the Lord. These are what the glorified Christ wanted to talk about most.

I am not advocating melodrama or theatrics that work up emotion. But I am in favor, as were the apostles, of asking God to stretch out his hand and manifest himself.

> **When a new Christian stands up and tells**
> **how God has revolutionized his or her life,**
> **no one dozes off.** ❧

People pay attention when they see that God actually changes persons and sets them free. When a new Christian stands up and tells how God has revolutionized his or her life, no one dozes off. When someone is healed or released from a life-controlling bondage, everyone takes notice. These things bear witness to a God who is strong and alive.

Who Is Outside the Fort?

Maintaining doctrinal purity is good, but it is not the whole picture for a New Testament church. The apostles wanted to do much more than simply "hold the fort," as the old gospel song says. They asked God to empower them to move out and impact an entire culture.

In too many places where the Bible is being thumped and doctrine is being argued until three in the morning, the Spirit of that doctrine is missing. William Law, an English devotional writer of the early 1700s, wrote, "Read whatever chapter of Scripture you will, and be ever so delighted with it—yet it will leave you as poor, as empty and unchanged as it found you unless it has turned you wholly and solely to the Spirit of God, and brought you into full union with and dependence upon him."[1]

One way to recognize whether we suffer from this disconnection is to look at our concern for people who are dirty ... people who are "other" ... people who don't fit the core group's image. The idea that a church could be called just to serve yuppies or some other designated class is not found in the

New Testament. The ravages of sin are not pleasant—but they are what Jesus came to forgive and heal. "The Son of Man came to seek and to save what was lost" (Luke 19:10). The Spirit of God is a Spirit of mercy, of compassion, of reaching out.

> **In too many places where the Bible is being thumped and doctrine is being argued until three in the morning, the Spirit of that doctrine is missing.** ❦

Yet Christians often hesitate to reach out to those who are different. They want God to clean the fish before they catch them. If someone's gold ring is attached to an unusual body part, if the person doesn't smell the best, or if the skin color is not the same, Christians tend to hesitate. But think for a moment about *God* reaching out to *us*. If ever there was a "reach," that was it: the holy, pure Deity extending himself to us who were soiled, evil-hearted, unholy. God could have said, "You're so different from me, so distasteful, I would really rather not get too close to you." But he didn't say that. It was our very differentness that drew his hand of love.

Jesus didn't just speak the healing word to lepers from a distance of thirty yards. He *touched* them.

I shall never forget Easter Sunday 1992—the day that Roberta Langella gave her dramatic testimony, as I recounted in chapter 3. A homeless man was standing in the back of the church, listening intently.

At the end of the evening meeting I sat down on the edge of the platform, exhausted, as others continued to pray with those who had responded to Christ. The organist was playing quietly. I wanted to relax. I was just starting to unwind when I looked up to see this man, with shabby clothing and matted hair, standing in the center aisle about four rows back and waiting for permission to approach me.

I nodded and gave him a weak little wave of my hand. *Look at how this Easter Sunday is going to end*, I thought to myself. *He's going to hit me up for money.* That happens often in this church. *I'm so tired....*

When he came close, I saw that his two front teeth were missing. But more striking was his odor—the mixture of alcohol, sweat, urine, and garbage took my breath away. I have been around many street people, but this was the strongest stench I have ever encountered. I instinctively had to turn my head sideways to inhale, then look back in his direction while breathing out.

I asked his name.

"David," he said softly.

"How long have you been homeless, David?"

"Six years."

"Where did you sleep last night?"

"In an abandoned truck."

I had heard enough and wanted to get this over quickly. I reached for the money clip in my back pocket.

At that moment David put his finger in front of my face and said, "No, you don't understand—I don't want your money. I'm going to die out there. I want the Jesus that red-haired girl talked about."

I hesitated, then closed my eyes. *God, forgive me*, I begged. I felt soiled and cheap. Me, a minister of the gospel ... I had wanted simply to get rid of him, when he was crying out for the help of Christ I had just preached about. I swallowed hard as God's love flooded my soul.

David sensed the change in me. He moved toward me and fell on my chest, burying his grimy head against my white shirt and tie. Holding him close, I talked to him about

Jesus' love. These weren't just words; I felt them. I felt love for this pitiful young man. And that smell . . . I don't know how to explain it. It had almost made me sick, but now it became the most beautiful fragrance to me. I reveled in what had been repulsive just a moment ago.

The Lord seemed to say to me in that instant, *Jim, if you and your wife have any value to me, if you have any purpose in my work—it has to do with this odor. This is the smell of the world I died for.*

David surrendered to the Christ he heard about that night. We got him into a hospital detoxification unit for a week. We got his teeth fixed. He joined the Prayer Band right away. He spent the next Thanksgiving Day in our home. We invited him back for Christmas as well.

I will never forget his present to me. Inside a little box was . . . one handkerchief. It was all he could afford.

Today David heads up the maintenance department at the church, overseeing ten other employees. He is now married and a father. God is opening more and more doors for him to go out and give his testimony. When he speaks, his words have a weight and an impact that many ordained ministers would covet.

As Christians reach out to touch everyone, including the unlovely who are now everywhere in our society, God touches them, too—and revolutionizes their lives. Otherwise we would just be circling the wagons, busying ourselves with Bible studies among our own kind. There is no demonstration of God's power because we have closed ourselves off from the *need* for such demonstration.

Why do the greatest miracle stories seem to come from mission fields, either overseas or among the destitute here at home (the Teen Challenge outreach to drug addicts, for example)? Because the need is there. Christians are taking their sound doctrine and extending it to lives in chaos, which is what God has called us all to do.

Without this extension of compassion it is all too easy for Bible teachers and authors to grow haughty. We become proud of what we know. We are so impressed with our doctrinal orderliness that we become intellectually arrogant. We have the rules and theories all figured out while the rest of the world is befuddled and confused about God's truth ... poor souls.

Such an attitude takes the heart out of the very Word we preach. We end up with lots of doctrinal particulars, but very little happens that resembles the Bible we're teaching from. I am personally tired of hearing all the positions and teaching principles. Where are the crowds of new converts? Where are the joyful baptisms? Where are the vibrant prayer meetings?

Once again, William Law writes:

> We may take for a certain rule, that the more the divine nature and life of Jesus is manifest in us, and the higher our sense of righteousness and virtue, the more we shall pity and love those who are suffering from the blindness, disease, and death of sin. The sight of such people then, instead of raising in us a haughty contempt or holier-than-thou indignation, will rather fill us with such tenderness and compassion as when we see the miseries of a dread disease.[2]

Carol and I have found that unless God baptizes us with fresh outpourings of love, we would leave New York City *yesterday!* We don't live in this crowded, ill-mannered, violent city because we like it. Whenever I meet or read about a guy who has sexually abused a little girl, I'm tempted in my flesh to throw him out a fifth-story window. This isn't an easy place for love to flourish.

But Christ died for that man. What could ever change him? What could ever replace the lust and violence in his heart? He isn't likely to read the theological commentaries on my bookshelves. He desperately needs to be surprised by the power of a loving, almighty God.

If the Spirit is not keeping my heart in line with my doctrine, something crucial is missing. I can affirm the existence of Jesus Christ all I want, but in order to be effective, he must come alive in my life in a way that even the pedophile, the prostitute, and the pusher can see.

ART OR HEART?

IF WE DO NOT yearn and pray and expect God to stretch out his hand and do the supernatural, it will not happen. That is the simple truth of the matter. We must give him room to operate. If we go on, week after week, filling the time with religious lectures and nothing more, God has little opportunity in which to move.

So long as we are busy polishing our oratory, the stage is entirely ours. Listen to the reproof of the great prophet of prayer E. M. Bounds more than a hundred years ago:

> Among the things that hinder spiritual results, fine preaching must have place among the first. Fine preaching is that kind of preaching where the force of the preacher is expended to make the sermon great in thought, tasteful as a work of art, perfect as a scholarly production, complete in rhetorical finish, and fine in its pleasing and popular force.
>
> In true preaching, the sermon proceeds out of the man. It is part of him, flowing out of his life. Fine preaching separates between the man and the sermon.

Such sermons will make an impression, but it is not the impression that the Holy Ghost makes. Influence it may have, but the influence is not distinctly spiritual, if spiritual at all. These sermons do not reach the conscience, are not even aimed at it.[3]

God is not nearly as enamored with the performance of pulpiteering as he is with humble words that manifest his presence to the soul. Consider Paul and Barnabas's ministry in two adjacent towns, as related in Acts 14:

1. Iconium: "Paul and Barnabas spent considerable time there, *speaking boldly* for the Lord, who *confirmed the message of his grace by enabling them to do miraculous signs and wonders*" (v. 3, italics added).

2. Lystra: "A man crippled in his feet ... listened to Paul as he was speaking. Paul looked directly at him, saw that he had faith to be healed and called out, 'Stand up on your feet!' At that, the man jumped up and began to walk" (vv. 8–10). The crowd's reaction was immediate.

Message plus divine demonstration. Doctrine plus power. This is the New Testament way.

For a more sobering example, see what happened in the previous chapter when these two apostles were addressing a government official on the island of Cyprus who "wanted to hear the word of God" (Acts 13:7). A sorcerer named Elymas interrupted the proclamation of the truth. "Paul, filled with the Holy Spirit, looked straight at Elymas" (v. 9) and rebuked him, announcing that God would strike him blind.

It is not accidental that the writer mentions Paul's spiritual condition: he was filled with the Holy Spirit. Here was a man specially empowered that moment by the Spirit and ready for the satanic challenge. Paul's doctrine was immediately reinforced by God's overwhelming power. "When the proconsul saw what had happened, he believed, for he was amazed at the teaching about the Lord" (Acts 13:12).

Amazed at the *teaching?* Yes, for this was a teaching with power. People must not only hear but feel, see, and experience the grace of God we speak about.

Such an event was certainly unpredictable. As we open up our church meetings to God's power, they will not always follow a predetermined schedule or order. Who can outline what God might have in mind?

As we open up our church meetings to God's power, they will not always follow a predetermined schedule. Who can outline what God might have in mind? ❧

Some have said, "The miracles, signs, and wonders of the book of Acts were temporary. They served to authenticate the apostles until such time as the New Testament could be written. Now we have the completed Word of God, which erases the need for supernatural happenings."

My response is this: If we have a completed revelation in written form, are we seeing at least as much advance for God's kingdom, as many people coming to Christ, as many victories over Satan as those poor fellows who had to get along with just the Old Testament? If not, why not? Are we missing something valuable that they felt was essential?

I have met preachers who have punched up a computer file and proudly showed me what they would be preaching for nearly the next year. Everything was cut-and-dried. The pressure of having to seek God week by week had been removed. What if God has a different idea? What if the spiritual temperature of the congregation changes by next

October? Without an anointing and prophetic edge to declare something fresh from God's Word, church life can be reduced to little more than a lecture series.

Imagine that Carol and I invited you to our home for a cookout. When you arrive, I greet you at the door. As soon as I take your coat, I hand you a little piece of paper with the evening's outline. There you see that for the first seven minutes we will have light socializing: How was the traffic? What are your kids doing these days?

Then for the next four minutes I will give a quick tour of our home, the deck out back, and so forth. Following that will be twenty-two minutes for the meal. The blessing will be voiced by Carol; then we will pass the food....

You would say to yourself, *This is weird! Why all the regimen? Can't we just relax and get to know one another? What if somebody has an idea or wants to talk about something that's not on the agenda?*

Too often a church service, which is meant to draw us toward God, is not all that much different. Spontaneity and the leading of the Spirit have been thrown out in the name of keeping things on schedule. However, there has never been a revival of religion so long as the order of service has been strictly followed.

Please understand: I am not campaigning for disorder. I am not saying "anything goes." I am asking us to remember that we are to be led by the Holy Spirit. Jesus said *he* would build his church, and we must not be so independent that we lose contact with the Master Planner. God the Holy Spirit does unusual things, and he does not always notify us in advance.

"Those who are led by the Spirit of God are sons of God," says Romans 8:14. Read the gospels and look for Jesus' daily agenda. It just isn't there. Scan the book of Acts to find the apostolic liturgy. You'll come up empty. What you will find are people moving in spontaneous obedience as they are propelled by the fresh wind of the Holy Spirit.

The prayer of the Jerusalem believers recorded in Acts 4 says in essence, "God, please don't send us out there alone just talking. Work with us; confirm your message in a supernatural way." What way and in what manner was left entirely (and rightly) to God alone.

Charles Finney, the lawyer turned evangelist, once said that as long as an audience kept looking at him while he preached, he knew he was failing. Only when their heads began to drop in deep conviction of sin did he know that God was working alongside him, producing a heart change inside. The words of sound doctrine alone were not enough.

In fact, revivals have never been dominated by eloquent or clever preaching. If you had timed the meetings with a stopwatch, you would have found far more minutes given to prayer, weeping, and repentance than to sermons. In the "Prayer Meeting Revival" of 1857–59 there was virtually no preaching at all. Yet it apparently produced the greatest harvest of any spiritual awakening in American history: estimates run to 1,000,000 converts across the United States, out of a national population at that time of only 30,000,000. That would be proportionate to *9,000,000 Americans today* falling on their knees in repentance!

How did this happen? A quiet businessman named Jeremiah Lanphier started a Wednesday noon prayer meeting in a Dutch Reformed church here in New York City, no more than a quarter mile from Wall Street. The first week, six people showed up. The next week, twenty came. The next week, forty … and they decided to have daily meetings instead.

"There was no fanaticism, no hysteria, just an incredible movement of people to pray," reports J. Edwin Orr. "The services were not given over to preaching. Instead, *anyone* was free to pray."[4]

During the fourth week, the financial Panic of 1857 hit; the bond market crashed, and the first banks failed. (Within a month, more than 1,400 banks had collapsed.) People began calling out to God more seriously than ever. Lanphier's church started having three noontime prayer meetings in different rooms. John Street Methodist Church, a few doors east of Broadway, was packed out as well. Soon Burton's Theater on Chambers Street was jammed with 3,000 people each noon.

The scene was soon replicated in Boston, New Haven, Philadelphia, Washington, and the South. By the next spring 2,000 Chicagoans were gathering each day in the Metropolitan Theater to pray. A young 21-year-old in those meetings, newly arrived in the city, felt his first call to do Christian work. He wrote his mother back East that he was going to start a Sunday school class. His name was Dwight L. Moody.

Does anyone really think that America today is lacking preachers, books, Bible translations, and neat doctrinal statements? What we really lack is the passion to call upon the Lord until he opens the heavens and shows himself powerful.

The Limits of Teaching

Let me make a bold statement: Christianity is not predominantly a teaching religion. We have been almost overrun these days by the cult of the speaker. The person who can stand up and expound correct doctrine is viewed as essential; without such a talent the church would not know what to do. As I said in an earlier chapter, the North American church has made the sermon the centerpiece of the meeting, rather than the throne of grace, where God acts in people's lives.

The Jewish faith in Jesus' day was dominated by rabbis—teachers of the law. Their doctrine was thorough. Jesus told them, "You diligently study the Scriptures because you think that *by them* you possess eternal life. These are the Scriptures that testify about me, yet you refuse to come to me to have life" (John 5:39–40, italics added). They knew the written word of God very well, but not the living Word, even as he stood before them.

> **Christianity is not predominantly a teaching religion.... The teaching of sound doctrine is a prelude, if you will, to the supernatural.** 🐚

The Scriptures are not so much the goal as they are an arrow that points us to the life-changing Christ.

Unfortunately, the rabbis never did realize who was among them. In the last few days before his crucifixion, Jesus wept over the city as he said, "You did not recognize the time of your visitation" (Luke 19:44 NASB).

It is fine to explain *about* God, but far too few people today are experiencing the living Christ in their lives. We are not seeing God's visitation in our gatherings. We are not on the lookout for his outstretched hand.

The teaching of sound doctrine is a prelude, if you will, to the supernatural. It is also a guide, a set of boundaries to keep emotion and exuberance within proper channels.

But as Paul said, "The letter kills, but the Spirit gives life" (2 Cor. 3:6). If the Holy Spirit is not given an opening among us, if his work is not welcomed, if we are afraid of what he might do, we leave ourselves with nothing but death.

Granted, extremists have done fanatical things in the name of the Holy Spirit that have frightened many sincere Christians away. Chaotic meetings with silly things going on and a lack of reverence for God have driven many to prefer a quiet, orderly lecture. But this is just another tactic of the enemy to make us throw out the baby with the bathwater. Satan's tendency is always to push us toward one extreme or the other: deadness or fanaticism.

Gordon D. Fee, a New Testament scholar whose heritage is Pentecostal, has said about corporate worship, "You really should have this incredible sense of unworthiness—'I don't really belong here'—coupled with the opposing sense of total joy—'It is all of grace, so I *do* belong here.' What bothers me about some within the Pentecostal and charismatic tradition is the joy without reverence, without awe." But in too many mainstream evangelical churches, Fee adds, there is neither "reverence *nor* joy."[5]

The old saying is true: If you have only the Word, you dry up. If you have only the Spirit, you blow up. But if you have both, you grow up.

We must not succumb to fear of the Holy Spirit. More than 200 years ago, William Law bluntly declared that the church of his day was "in the same apostasy that characterized the Jewish nation.... The Jews refused Him who was the substance and fulfilling of all that was taught in their Law and Prophets. The Christian church is in a fallen state for the same rejection of the Holy Spirit." He said further that just as the Jews refused Jesus and quoted Scripture to prove their point, "so church leaders today reject the demonstration and power of the Holy Spirit in the name of sound doctrine."[6]

What would the Englishman say if he were alive today?

A Cry for More

I DO NOT MEAN to imply that all is well-adjusted in the life and worship of the Brooklyn Tabernacle. As I said in the beginning, there are no perfect churches. I must be honest and tell you that I live with an almost constant sense of failure. When I think of what God could do for all the needs of this city and how little we are accomplishing, it makes me passionate to seek God's intervention in even more powerful ways.

North American Christians must no longer accept the status quo. No more neat little meetings, even with the benefit of 100 percent correct doctrine.

Are we hiding behind the doctrine of God's omnipresence, that he is everywhere around the globe, especially "where two or three are gathered together" ... to the point that we don't seriously ask and expect to see him work with power in our lives *here and now?* Shouldn't we expect to *see* him in action once in a while? Shouldn't we implore him to manifest himself? Moses did. Joshua did. Elijah did. Elisha did. Peter did. Philip did. Paul did. Shouldn't we?

God will manifest himself in direct proportion to our passion for him. The principle he laid down long ago is still true: "You will seek me and find me when you seek me with all your heart" (Jer. 29:13). *O God, split the heavens and come down! Manifest yourself somehow. Do what only you can do.*

PART 3

❦

The Road Ahead

TEN

❦

Too Smart for
Our Own Good?

OFTEN WHEN OUR PASTORAL staff meets together, amid the
flurry of busy days and what the world would term "church
success"—a large membership, nearly twenty branch
churches, the choir performing at Billy Graham crusades, our
videos being televised nationwide, invitations to speak here
and there—a nagging thought from the Lord spreads across
the edges of our hearts: *Remember who has done all this. Your
need for me hasn't lessened at all.*

If you have been a Christian for any length of time, the
same is true for you individually. Your first rush of emotion
at how God wonderfully saved you from sin has faded. Your
desperate early days when you cried out to the Lord because
you didn't know what you were doing (as I had to do back on
Atlantic Avenue) have given way to a degree of confidence
and assurance. You and I have learned a lot, seen and heard a
lot, built a track record, and accumulated a fair storehouse of
"wisdom."

That's why we are at great risk.

We discover what this means in the life of a man named
Asa. You probably haven't thought about this Old Testament
king in a long time—maybe never. Most readers of the Bible,
unless they happen to be history buffs, doze off once they

finish the accounts of the famous monarchs Saul, David, and Solomon.

Asa was Solomon's great-grandson. God gave him three whole chapters of 2 Chronicles for a reason. I happen to think his biography is one of the most important in all of Scripture, especially for today.

Asa was not brought up to be a spiritual person. Solomon, as everyone knows, had wandered from God near the end of his life. Rehoboam, who came next, and then Abijah, Asa's father, let idol worship come right into the midst of what was supposed to be a godly society. Baal was welcomed as a help to the crops; Asherah poles, oversized carvings of the male sex organ supposed to bring fertility, were common; children were actually offered as sacrifices in the fires of Molech.

In such a spiritual climate, who was it who got through to young Asa and convinced him to seek the Lord? We don't know. Second Chronicles 14:2–4 tells us only that early in his reign Asa "did what was good and right in the eyes of the LORD his God. He removed the foreign altars and the high places, smashed the sacred stones and cut down the Asherah poles. He commanded Judah to seek the LORD, the God of their fathers, and to obey his laws and commands."

In essence, Asa was saying, "Time out! We have a mess on our hands. The foreign altars and immorality must go. We're going to clean house throughout this entire kingdom. We're going to start obeying the Lord's commands and call out to him with all our hearts. We must have him near us in order to receive his blessing."

These people were Israelites, sons and daughters of Abraham, living in a specially chosen land. But they were in a terrible spiritual condition nonetheless. Their heritage did not remove the consequences of displeasing God. No claim of special rank could exempt them. In fact, their elect status would bring God's correction even more quickly than it would to their enemies.

The first step in any spiritual awakening is *demolition*. We cannot make headway in seeking God without first tearing down the accumulated junk in our souls. Rationalizing has to cease. We have to start seeing the sinful debris we hadn't noticed before, which is what holds back the blessing of God.

I wonder if any government employee said, "Excuse me, King Asa, but your father built that particular shrine.... Your grandfather dedicated that incense altar. Are you sure you want them demolished?"

If they had, Asa would have replied, "Tear them down— now! They're wrong. This idolatry was borrowed from the Canaanites—but we're not Canaanites. God will never bless us as long as these things stand."

Anytime people get hungry to truly know the Lord, the Holy Spirit quickly puts a shovel and broom into their hands. Husbands and wives begin to deal with long-buried issues hurting their marriages. Adults take a closer look at their choice of TV programs and movies. Church members begin to see the damage wreaked by their gossip, their racial attitudes, their criticism.

Anytime people get hungry to truly know the Lord, the Holy Spirit quickly puts a shovel and broom into their hands. ✹

I admit this sounds old-fashioned. I am out of step with the modern habit of "claiming" God's blessing regardless of how we live. But what does the Bible show us?

Sin grieves the Holy Spirit and quenches his power among us. Without his blessing we miss out on what God has for us and wants us to be, no matter what religious label we may be carrying.

One Sunday about 20 years ago, back in our days in the YWCA, I said something impromptu while receiving new members into the church that has stuck with us ever since. People were standing in a row across the front before me, and as I spoke, the Holy Spirit seemed to prompt me to add, "And now, I charge you, as pastor of this church, that if you ever hear another member speak an unkind word of criticism or slander against anyone—myself, another pastor, an usher, a choir member, or anyone else—you have authority to stop that person in midsentence and say, 'Excuse me—who hurt you? Who ignored you? Who slighted you? Was it Pastor Cymbala? Let's go to his office right now. He will get on his knees and apologize to you, and then we'll pray together, so God can restore peace to this body. But we will not let you talk critically about people who are not present to defend themselves.'

"New members, please understand that I am entirely serious about this. I want you to help resolve this kind of thing immediately. And meanwhile, know this: If *you* are ever the one doing the loose talking, we will confront you."

To this very day, every time we receive new members, I say much the same thing. It is always a solemn moment. That is because I know what most easily destroys churches. It is not crack cocaine. It is not government oppression. It is not even lack of funds. Rather, it is gossip and slander that grieves the Holy Spirit.

People nod their heads with understanding, and as a result, rumor and busybody talk are kept to a minimum. We have had to confront a few people along the way, of course, but the general concern to live with clean hearts and clean speech before the Lord prevents many problems from ever getting started.

Asa's early years were marked by a national housecleaning. God's blessing flowed upon the king and his people in response.

A GREAT CHALLENGE

UNFORTUNATELY, SEEKING THE LORD wholeheartedly does not exempt us from outside attack. After ten years of peace, Asa's corner of the world was suddenly invaded by a huge Cushite (Ethiopian) army for no apparent reason. Asa's godliness did not guarantee a smooth road for the rest of his life.

> **Unfortunately, seeking the Lord wholeheartedly does not exempt us from outside attack.** ❧

In such a moment, seekers after God have built up a reservoir of ready faith to meet new problems. They know exactly what to do:

"Asa called to the LORD his God and said, 'LORD, there is no one like you to help the powerless against the mighty. Help us, O LORD our God, for we rely on you, and in your name we have come against this vast army. O LORD, you are our God; do not let man prevail against you'" (2 Chron. 14:11).

Asa's faith was not some kind of instant cake mix stirred from a box on the pantry shelf. He and the people had already been calling out to God for a decade. Hence, there was no panic. They cried for the Lord to arise—and he did. The Cushites were decisively wiped out, despite their overwhelming numbers, "for the terror of the LORD had fallen upon them" (v. 14).

This is a classic example of a cardinal principle of God's dealing with humanity. Hebrews 11:6 expresses it best:

"Anyone who comes to [God] must believe that he exists and that *he rewards those who earnestly seek him.*" I cannot say it strongly enough: When we seek God, he *will* bless us. But when we stop seeking him . . . all bets are off, no matter who we are. It doesn't matter how much talent we have, how many diplomas hang on our walls, what word of prophecy was proclaimed over us, or anything else.

On Asa's way home from the battle, a prophet stopped him and his army along the road to reinforce what had just happened:

"Listen to me. . . . The LORD is with you when you are with him. If you seek him, he will be found by you, but if you forsake him, he will forsake you" (2 Chron. 15:2). The cause-and-effect relationship could not be clearer.

The more we seek God, the more we see our need to seek him. Asa, buoyed by this experience, began to look around . . . and discovered things he had missed earlier. The altar in God's temple was broken down; he immediately ordered it repaired. He called a solemn assembly of the whole population, where he made a new covenant with God.

> **God did not call me to be a white middle-class Christian; he called me to be a Christian, period.** ❧

He was later shocked to find that his own grandmother, Maacah, still had "a repulsive Asherah pole" (15:16). He cut down the pole and deposed the elderly woman from her throne as queen mother. Can you believe that Asa had the nerve to bust his own grandmother! The people of the land could not help but say to one another, "This king is *serious* about pleasing God."

Imagine the social current he was up against. Imagine the emotional ties he had to sever. His whole sense of family allegiance was arrayed against God's will. But Asa was determined to be more than just "Maacah's grandson."

I see many churchgoers today who find family pressure too much to challenge. Others are caught up with being part of the middle-class scene, or with being white, or black. God did not call me to be a white middle-class Christian; he called me to be a Christian, period, and whatever he asks takes precedence over every other loyalty.

Even being an American is not of the same magnitude with being a seeker after God. Preserving the American culture cannot be allowed to compete with advancing God's kingdom. Whatever God approves of comes first. Whatever grieves him has to go.

We are always either drawing nearer to God or falling away. There is no holding pattern. 🌿

Asa understood who deserved his first loyalty. It was not his grandmother, his culture, his tradition, or anything else. It was God alone. What a wonderful example of single-hearted service to the Lord!

THE BLUNDER

I WOULD GIVE ANYTHING if Asa's story ended this way. It doesn't.

Twenty-five years went by. Somewhere along the way—as has happened to many churches, pastors, choir directors, and whole denominations—Asa *stopped feeling his need to seek the Lord.* We don't know why. We don't know whether the cares of life somehow made him spiritually soft. Maybe he thought he had reached a spiritual pinnacle and could relax. But the Bible teaches that we are always either drawing nearer to God or falling away. There is no holding pattern.

One day Asa received news that a *small* army from his northern neighbor was starting to build a blockade around his territory (see 2 Chron. 16). The opponent was not nearly the size of the Cushite horde of a quarter century earlier. What would Asa do now? How would he respond?

"Asa then took the silver and gold out of the treasuries of the LORD's temple and of his own palace and sent it to Ben-Hadad king of Aram, who was ruling in Damascus. 'Let there be a treaty between me and you,' he said" (vv. 2–3).

This is stranger than Ripley's Believe It or Not. The man who had built his whole success in life upon seeking after God was now dipping into the Lord's coffers for a secular buy-off!

And the king of Aram was willing to be bought. He sent his army to put pressure on Asa's enemy, who quickly backed away from attacking Jerusalem. Asa even got to capture some building materials that were left behind.

In other words, the plan "worked." Asa probably felt proud of himself. *I used my head and figured my way out of this one. I'm smart.*

The people realized they had a very clever leader. Many churches today are making the same assumption: Whatever "works" is the way to go. If a technique gets the building filled and the bills paid, it must be blessed by God. Visible results are the proof that a strategy is heaven-ordained. Such thinking is due for a rude awakening when we stand before the Lord.

While Asa's court officials were high-fiving each other on the brilliant maneuver just completed ... in walked another prophet, named Hanani. He began to speak, and faces suddenly dropped.

"Because you relied on the king of Aram and not on the LORD your God, the army of the king of Aram has escaped from your hand...." (v. 7). In other words, there would be no way for Asa ever to oppose Aram in the future; he was locked into being cooperative with this pagan empire.

God's messenger pressed on:

"Were not the Cushites and Libyans a mighty army with great numbers of chariots and horsemen? Yet when you relied on the LORD, he delivered them into your hand. *For the eyes of the LORD range throughout the earth to strengthen those whose hearts are fully committed to him.* You have done a foolish thing, and from now on you will be at war" (vv. 8–9, italics added).

Today God's eyes are still running all across America, Canada, Mexico, the islands of the sea, the world ... looking for someone—*anyone*—who will totally and passionately seek him, who is determined that every thought and action will be pleasing in his sight. For such a person or group, God will prove himself mighty. His power will explode on their behalf.

Day after day goes by, and God keeps looking, looking.... Doesn't anyone want to call out for his blessing? Upon whom can he pour his grace? Isn't anyone interested?

The less we look for God, the more he has to go looking for us. Why not run in his direction? When Jesus cried out in the middle of the temple crowd in Jerusalem, he said, "If anyone is thirsty, let him come to me and drink. Whoever believes in me, as the Scripture has said, streams of living water will flow from within him" (John 7:37).

When we align ourselves with the channel of God's living grace, all kinds of marvelous things take place. His power energizes us to face any army, large or small, and win victories for him. We call upon him, and he sends us forth to accomplish what we could never do alone, regardless of our money, education, or track record.

Tough to the End

I WISH I COULD tell you that Asa fell on his knees and begged God's forgiveness for straying, for thinking up his own political solution instead of calling upon the Lord. I wish I could say that Asa's heart melted in confession, resulting in a return to the fervent faith of his younger days.

In fact, the opposite happened.

"Asa was angry with the seer because of this; he was so enraged that he put him in prison. At the same time Asa brutally oppressed some of the people" (2 Chron. 16:10).

The young king who once led a whole nation in seeking God now became a coldhearted oppressor of that nation. Asa's story illustrates how people who stop seeking God tend to get crusty and arrogant. They think they know everything. A prophetic rebuke only irritates them.

Compare Asa with his great-great-grandfather, David, who in his later years made mistakes, too. In fact, David's blunders were even worse: a one-night stand with a married woman, a follow-up murder of her husband, later on, an unwise census. But when rebuked by prophets—Nathan in one case, Gad in the other—David broke down. "I have sinned greatly in what I have done," he confessed (2 Sam. 24:10). Psalm 51 is an eloquent, emotional outpouring of guilt before the Lord. No wonder he was called "a man after God's own heart."

People who have a seeking heart still make mistakes. But their reaction to rebuke and correction shows the condition of that heart. It determines what God is able to do with them in the future.

> **People who have a seeking heart still make mistakes. But their reaction to rebuke and correction shows the condition of that heart. ❧**

If Asa, like David, had broken before God, who knows how his life would have ended? But he did not, and the closing picture of Asa is downright pitiful. As an old man he developed a painful case of foot trouble, probably gout. He hobbled around his palace, every step bringing a grimace to his face. "Though his disease was severe, even in his illness he did not seek help from the LORD, but only from the physicians. Then in the forty-first year of his reign Asa died" (2 Chron. 16:12–13).

Christendom, like Asa, is suffering from major illness today. Our vital signs are not good. Now we face a choice. We can stay hard and justify our backsliding by saying, "Don't tell me my spiritual life needs correction. I'm getting along; everything is still 'working,' isn't it? Leave me alone." Or we can be like David and admit the truth.

Anything and everything is possible with God if we approach him with a broken spirit. We must humble ourselves, get rid of the debris in our lives, and keep leaning on him instead of our own understanding. Your future and mine are determined by this one thing: seeking after the Lord. The blessings we receive and then pass along to others all hang on this truth: "He rewards those who earnestly seek him" (Heb. 11:6).

ELEVEN

※

In Search of
Ordinary Heroes

THERE WILL COME A DAY when faith becomes sight, and then—only then—will our seeking of the Lord be finished at last. We will find ourselves in heaven, standing face-to-face with the One we have trusted and followed for so long. He himself will be what makes it truly heaven—not streets of gold or walls of jasper, but God alone in all his splendor. We will know him as he has known us from the beginning.

In addition, what a delight it will be to meet those heroes of the faith, both men and women, who fill the pages of the Bible. I can't wait to greet Paul the apostle, who penned so much of the New Testament and whose life has inspired so many Christians. I long to talk with Moses, who led Israel out of Egypt and did great exploits for God. Then I will soon move along to Abraham, Deborah, Joshua, Ruth, David, Helez, Sibbecai, Ahiam, Hezro, Zabad . . . *Who? Did I wander off track a bit? You say you don't recognize those last few names?*

They are all carefully listed in 1 Chronicles 11, an amazing group of warriors known as David's "mighty men." God the Holy Spirit thought they were impressive enough to have every last one written down, because "they, together with all Israel, gave [David's] kingship strong support to extend it over the whole land, as the LORD had promised" (v. 10).

Such individuals are role models for us today—even if we can't pronounce their names. Some names are a bit strange, I admit: "Elhanan son of Dodo" (v. 26). I assume this father's name didn't mean the same thing in Hebrew as it does in English! While some young parents these days are enamored with choosing Old Testament names such as Seth or Caleb for their new baby boys, I doubt there will ever be a comeback for those in this list: Ithai, Hepher, Mibhar, Uzzia....

Nevertheless, these are people who applied their strength and courageous action toward what God had promised. It was not enough for them that the prophet Samuel had anointed David king-in-waiting back when he was a teenager. Much more recently the elders of Israel had gathered in Hebron to declare David the new monarch. But out in the villages, and especially on the borders of the land, not everyone was convinced. The picture was still unclear. The rule of God's king was yet to be established. Foreign enemies were still living inside the land promised to God's people.

These heroes did not just sit back, as many do today, saying, "Well, God promised, and I'm sure he'll fulfill his word." They stepped up and took action to make the promise become reality. They understood that God's work in the world is usually a joint project; he works with us as we yield ourselves to work with him.

So these men risked their lives. They left their families and headed for dangerous territory. The Bible uses a special word three times to describe what they did: *"exploits"* (vv. 19, 22, 24).

Similarly, the gospel of Jesus Christ will be planted today in hostile cities and territories and nations only by mighty men and women who dare to take risks. Apathetic churches across the land will be revived only by people of deep spirituality who refuse to accept the status quo. Wayward children and broken marriages will be touched by the hand of God only as someone stands in the gap and fights valiantly in the power of the Spirit.

Among the mighty warriors I have had the privilege of knowing, I count Delores Bonner, an African-American woman who lives alone in Bedford-Stuyvesant, one of Brooklyn's toughest neighborhoods. She has been a medical technician at Maimonides Hospital for more than thirty years. Carol and I met her one year at Christmastime while we were bringing gifts to some poor children in our congregation.

Delores had a full apartment that day—but these children were not hers. She had brought them from a nearby shelter to meet us. Their natural mother was too consumed with her own problems to be present even for an occasion such as this.

"How did you come to meet these children?" I asked.

She modestly mumbled something that didn't really answer my question. Only from others did I learn that right after her conversion in a prayer meeting at the church in 1982, she became concerned for children in the streets and in the crack houses. God touched her heart, and she started bringing the children to Sunday school. At first she packed them into taxis; later on someone heard what she was doing and bought her a car. Today she has a van so she can transport more children and teenagers to hear the gospel.

This is only part of Delores's story. On Sundays between services, she oversees the crew that cleans the sanctuary so it will be ready for the next crowd. On Saturdays she goes out with the evangelism teams, knocking on doors in the housing projects to share God's love. On weekdays I find her on her knees upstairs with the Prayer Band, taking a shift to intercede for people's needs. She did the same thing on a ministry trip to Peru, where she joined others in calling out to God on my behalf as I preached in an outdoor meeting.

When we honored Delores as the Brooklyn Tabernacle's "Woman of the Year," she was embarrassed and said little. But the whole church knows that living among us is a mighty woman of God whose fame transcends the world's shallow value system.

Delores is a woman of quiet determination, the kind shown in 1 Chronicles 12:18, where it says, "The Spirit came upon Amasai, chief of the Thirty, and he said: 'We are yours, O David! We are with you, O son of Jesse! Success, success [or "peace and prosperity"] to you, and success to those who help you, *for your God will help you.*" Once again, the merging of divine and human effort is clearly shown.

Oddly, two people on David's list weren't even Jewish. They would never have been allowed to worship at the holy tabernacle. Zelek the Ammonite (1 Chron. 11:39) and Ithmah the Moabite (v. 46) were definitely from the "wrong" nationalities. Their countrymen harassed the Israelites continually and tempted them toward idolatry. Yet Zelek and Ithmah ended up being honored because they fought and risked their lives for God's king.

All these were common people who did uncommon things for God. In that sense, they remind us of those "unschooled, ordinary" people of Acts 4:13, of whom we have already said much. David's thirty mighty warriors were not royalty. They were not graduates of West Point or Annapolis. They were just regular people from small places—Anathoth, Tekoa, Gibeah—who set their hearts to do exploits for God's anointed one.

What we desperately need in our own time are not Christians full of cant and posturing, railing at the world's problems of secular humanism, New Age, or whatever. We need men and women who will step out to turn back today's slide toward godlessness, prayerless churches, family breakup,

and waning evangelistic fervor. They may not have been to
seminary, but they have been schooled and trained by God
for hand-to-hand warfare in the spiritual realm.

THE TELLING MOMENT

THE FIRST PERSON ON David's list, Jashobeam, "raised his
spear against three hundred men, whom he killed in one
encounter" (1 Chron. 11:11). That sounds impossible. There
is no way he could pile up that kind of body count without
the overshadowing presence and power of God. Human
bravery alone is not enough when the odds are 300 to 1.

When it comes to spiritual matters, you and I will never
know our potential under God until we step out and take
risks on the front line of battle. We will never see what power
and anointing are possible until we bond with our King and
go out in his name to establish his kingdom. Sitting safely in
the shelter of Bible discussions among ourselves, or com-
plaining to one another about the horrible state of today's
society, does nothing to unleash the power of God. He meets
us in the moment of battle. He energizes us when there is an
enemy to be pushed back.

> **You and I will never know our potential under
> God until we step out and take risks on the
> front line of battle.** ❧

In verses 12–14 we meet Eleazar, who accompanied
David into a major battle with the Philistines. We get an idea
of how formidable the enemy was when the Bible says, "At a
place where there was a field full of barley, the troops fled
from the Philistines." This was no minor skirmish; this was

all-out combat against a superior opponent. Many frightened Israelite soldiers saw the coming horde and ran for their lives.

But not Eleazar. He and David "took their stand in the middle of the field. They defended it and struck the Philistines down, and the LORD brought about a great victory." Once again we see the combination of human and divine efforts. God did not act alone. He didn't unleash a lightning strike from heaven to fry the Philistines. Instead, he was looking all across the horizon that day to see who would stay in the barley field and thus receive his supernatural aid. While others left in fear, these two—David and Eleazar—stood firm.

The account in 2 Samuel 23:10 adds even more detail about Eleazar. He "stood his ground and struck down the Philistines till his hand grew tired and froze to the sword." He swung his weapon with such grit, such adrenaline, that his muscles locked up on him; he couldn't let go. Talk about a mighty warrior for God!

What the world's situation cries out for today is this kind of determined and desperate faith that grips the sword of the Spirit, which is the Word of God, and won't let go until victory comes.

A man such as Eleazar brings to mind the little-known, seldom-seen partner of the great evangelist Charles Finney during the Second Great Awakening. His name was Daniel Nash, and he had had a lackluster record as a pastor in upstate New York. He finally decided, at the age of forty-eight, to give himself totally to prayer for Finney's meetings.

"Father Nash," as some called him, would quietly slip into a town three or four weeks before Finney's arrival, rent a room, find two or three other like-minded Christians to join him, and start pleading with God. In one town the best he could find was a dark, damp cellar; it became his center for intercession.

In another place, Finney relates,

> When I got to town to start a revival a lady contacted me who ran a boarding house. She said, "Brother Finney, do you know a Father Nash? He and two other men have been at my boarding house for the last three days, but they haven't eaten a bite of food. I opened the door and peeped in at them because I could hear them groaning, and I saw them down on their faces. They have been this way for three days, lying prostrate on the floor and groaning. I thought something awful must have happened to them. I was afraid to go in and I didn't know what to do. Would you please come see about them?"
>
> "No, it isn't necessary," I replied. "They just have a spirit of travail in prayer."[1]

Once the public meetings began, Nash usually did not attend. He kept praying in his hideaway for the conviction of the Holy Spirit to melt the crowd. If opposition arose—as it often did in those rugged days of the 1820s—Finney would tell him about it, and Father Nash would bear down all the harder in prayer.

One time a group of young men openly announced that they were going to break up the meetings. Nash, after praying, came out of the shadows to confront them. "Now, mark me, young men! God will break your ranks in less than one week, either by converting some of you, or by sending some of you to hell. He will do this as certainly as the Lord is my God!"

Finney admits that at that point he thought his friend had gone over the edge. But the next Tuesday morning, the leader of the group suddenly showed up. He broke down before Finney, confessed his sinful attitude, and gave himself to Christ.

"What shall I do, Mr. Finney?" he asked then. The evangelist sent him back to tell his companions what had changed in his life. Before the week was out, "nearly if not all of that class [group] of young men were hoping in Christ," Finney reported.[2]

In 1826 a mob in a certain town burned effigies of the two: Finney and Nash. These unbelievers recognized that one man was as big a threat to their wickedness as the other.

Shortly before Nash died in the winter of 1831, he wrote in a letter,

> I am now convinced, it is my duty and privilege, and the duty of every other Christian, to pray for as much of the Holy Spirit as came down on the day of Pentecost, and a great deal more.... My body is in pain, but I am happy in my God.... I have only just begun to understand what Jesus meant when He said, "All things whatsoever ye shall ask in prayer, believing, ye shall receive."[3]

Within four months of Nash's death, Finney left the itinerant field to become the pastor of a church in New York City. His partner in cracking the gates of hell was gone. If you want to see Father Nash's grave today, you will have to drive to northern New York, almost to the Canadian border. There, in a neglected cemetery along a dirt road, you will find a tombstone that says it all:

DANIEL NASH
Laborer with Finney
Mighty in Prayer
Nov. 17, 1775–Dec. 20, 1831

Daniel Nash was a nobody to the elite of his time. They would have found this humble man not worthy of comment because he lived on a totally different plane. But you can be sure that he was known all too well in both heaven and hell.

The Bible tells about another Daniel whose dedication made an impression in the courts of God. "A hand touched me and set me trembling on my hands and knees. He said, 'Daniel, *you who are highly esteemed ...*'" (Dan. 10:10, italics added). Imagine being acclaimed by heaven itself!

God's mighty men and women lay aside the distractions of life to do exploits in the spiritual realm. Whether or not they become famous is beside the point. 🌿

This is how it is with all God's mighty men and women. They are famous in heaven; they win crowns that make all earth's riches seem like cheap tinsel. They may witness, teach, lead, and pray in obscurity on earth, but they are the talk of heaven.

In every century, on every continent, warriors such as these are the ones who press forward the kingdom of God. They lay aside the distractions of life to do exploits in the spiritual realm. Whether or not they become famous on earth is beside the point. They are heroes and heroines nonetheless.

WHO, US?

THE LIST OF DAVID'S mighty warriors in 1 Chronicles 11:22 introduces us to Benaiah, whose exploits included overcoming two of Moab's best men. He also killed a lion in a snowy, slippery pit. Perhaps most amazingly, he took on an Egyptian tall enough to be a starting center for the Chicago Bulls. This seven-and-a-half-foot giant wielded a spear with a shaft as sturdy as a lead pipe while Benaiah had only a wooden club.

Even so . . . Benaiah "snatched the spear from the Egyptian's hand and killed him with his own spear. Such were the exploits of Benaiah son of Jehoiada. . . . He was held in greater honor than any of the Thirty" (vv. 23–25).

It was not a Ph.D. degree that brought honor to a person in those days. Honor did not necessarily flow to the person with money or leverage or media access. Honor came as a result of doing exploits for the king.

Who is doing exploits for God today? Where is the enemy being driven back? That is the great yearning of all spiritually minded people. They are not enchanted with polished sermons and slick organizational technique. Where are the mighty men and women anointed by God to truly make a difference?

> **Who is doing exploits for God today? Where is the enemy being driven back?** *

I think I know at least one of God's mighty people. Rina Gatdula, a Filipino lady, is like a sister to Carol and me. God sent her in the early days of the Brooklyn Tabernacle with a valiant spirit that proved to be a tremendous blessing. When our ushers were intimidated by the occasional drunk or hostile person who would wander in, Rina would confront him or her head-on with a fearlessness granted by the Holy Spirit.

Although not especially gifted as a public speaker, she had a ministry of prayer and intercession that helped to carry us through many battles. Whether it is the need for a larger building or the need for a backslider to return to the Lord, she has the spirit of Benaiah. She will not let go of God when needy people come to the altar seeking help. She knows the fine art of "praying through" with people; many have found deliverance in Christ because she has stood with them at the throne of grace.

Her tenacity is so unique that when she moved to another part of the country, churches there almost didn't know what to make of her. They didn't understand her gifts; they saw only that her English was limited and that she didn't have certain clever skills. As a result, they didn't open up to her ministry.

Today Rina travels among the churches the Brooklyn Tabernacle has begun, both in this country and overseas, reminding them of the exploits they can do through God. She always seems to spark a spirit of prayer. Whether in Harlem, San Francisco, or Lima, Peru, she is a living example of a heroine of faith.

Consider how many gospel-preaching churches there are in the fifty states of America—200,000, if not more. If each of these churches, on average, brought only two converts to Christ a week—not robbing people from First Baptist or First Nazarene down the road, but winning new people for the kingdom of God—that would mean 100 new baptized believers in each church in a year's time, *or 20,000,000 nationwide*.

The population of the entire United States is about 270,000,000. By merely bringing eight or nine people a month to Christ in each church, America would be dramatically changed within two to three years. Can any serious Bible-preaching church not take on this modest goal in the name of its King?

God's plan for the local church has always centered in evangelism. Those brought to Christ are thus born into the very place where they can be nurtured and discipled. This avoids the slippage we often see when parachurch ministries try to do the work mainly assigned to the local church.

An evangelistic focus, of course, would force us back to serious prayer and an emphasis on the simple gospel of Jesus

Christ. God would prepare us as only he can for victorious spiritual warfare. Concerned believers wouldn't have time to watch as much television as they do now. A lot of other activities would have to give way. Living in the Bible, calling upon the Lord, fasting, and then reaching out to the unsaved would consume us. We would require God's anointing, whatever the cost.

Some churches in very small towns might have trouble reaching 100 people per year, but they would be offset by churches in urban areas, where the need and the opportunity are so great.

If the American church actually set out to do this "exploit" for God, bringing 20,000,000 to Christ this year, another 20,000,000 next year . . . in three or four years we wouldn't recognize our culture. Broadway and Hollywood would have to acknowledge the shift in audience preferences. Abortion clinics would wonder where all their customers went. Drug abuse would plummet.

Some will accuse me of idealistic dreaming, but isn't this plan the last thing Jesus told us to fulfill before his ascension? "Go and make disciples of all nations," he said, "baptizing them in the name of the Father and of the Son and of the Holy Spirit, and teaching them to obey everything I have commanded you" (Matt. 28:19–20). What will it take to shake denominational leaders, pastors, and laypeople, seeing that we all must answer to Christ at the Judgment Seat one day? Our sense of inadequacy is no excuse, given that he has promised to work with us as we set our hearts to the task of extending his kingdom.

Brave for God

The mighty warriors of 1 Chronicles 11 even helped David conquer a new capital for his kingdom, a story told in verses 4–9. The modern nation of Israel has made a big celebration of the 3,000th birthday of this city, Jerusalem, as the center of Jewish life.

It was not an easy prize. The Jebusites who lived in Jerusalem flatly told David, "No way. This is a tough, fortified city, and you won't get inside." In fact, 2 Samuel 5:6 records their insult: "Even the blind and the lame can ward you off."

So it is with every attempt to do something significant for God. It is never simple. Whenever God stirs us to establish his kingdom in a new place, the enemy is sure to taunt us. The devil always tries to convince us that we've tackled too much this time and we'll soon be humiliated.

But David and his warriors pressed on. They would not be turned back. In fact, David made an unusual offer: "Whoever leads the attack on the Jebusites will become commander-in-chief" (1 Chron. 11:6). This meant being the first to head uphill against well-armed soldiers perched atop thick walls, just waiting to rain down arrows and rocks. David's young nephew Joab, however, seized the opportunity to perform this exploit. He broke into the city first, and thus he became David's leading general for years to come.

That is not how we select leaders in the church today, is it? We go by resumes, seniority, image, education, and a half-dozen other human criteria. By contrast, David looked for bravery and boldness in the real world of battle.

If we are courageous enough to go on the spiritual attack, to be mighty men and women of prayer and faith, there is no limit to what God can accomplish through us. Some of us will turn out to be famous like King David and Catherine Booth and Charles Finney; the rest will remain obscure like Eleazar and Daniel Nash and Rina Gatdula. That doesn't matter. What counts is bringing God's power and light into a dark world, seeing local communities touched by God as churches turn back from perilous apathy to become Holy Spirit centers of divine activity.

The heroes of church history whom we now revere were not known for their cleverness; they were warriors for God. Moody was never ordained to the ministry. Finney never went to seminary. Yet whole cities were visited by God as a result of their anointed work.

The Time Is Now

What is it really that stops us from becoming mighty warriors in the Lord? God has not changed. He is still superior to anything the enemy can throw against us.

No personal or church situation is too hopeless for the all-sufficient power of the Holy Spirit. God will be no more eager to act tomorrow than he is right now. He is waiting for us to take his promises seriously and go boldly to the throne of grace. He wants us to meet the enemy at the very point of attack, standing against him in the name of Christ. When we do so, God will back us up with all the resources of heaven.

Dear Father, thank you for your mercy and the salvation you have given us in Jesus Christ. Please forgive us for all our sins and shortcomings. Draw us to you, and begin a new work of grace in all of us.

Make us the people you want us to be. Fill our churches with your fresh wind and fresh fire. Break our pride, soften our hearts, and fill us to overflowing with your Holy Spirit.

O God, do all this so that the name of Jesus will be exalted throughout the earth.

Amen.

A Word to Pastors

I HAVE ALWAYS STRUGGLED with the notion of addressing pastors, because I am keenly aware of my lack of classical training. But in the school of practical experience, the main truths of the Bible have become evident, and that is what I try to share.

I mention the following out of my heart's concern that all of us fulfill God's calling on our lives:

1. Every real pastor is in the ministry today because, in the words of Ephesians 4:11, "it was he [Christ] who gave some to be . . . pastors and teachers." The ministry was not your idea or mine; it was God's plan from the beginning of time. He has entrusted us with a sacred privilege, and with that comes an awesome responsibility—one for which we will have to answer at the Judgment Seat of Christ.

Let us all lead our congregations with the desire for divine acceptance, rather than focusing so much on current trends or what is popular with our peers. Christ will one day assess the *quality* of our work. He will pay no attention to trends set by others in the pastoral profession. That is why we all need to go humbly before him with open hearts, letting him rearrange all we do in order to meet his approval.

2. We must face the fact that for our churches and ministries to be all God wants them to be, they *must* be saturated with prayer. No new revelation or church-growth technique will change the fact that spiritual power is *always* linked to

communion with God. If you and I are prayerless, if our churches have no appetite for God's presence, we will never reach our full potential in him.

3. Many visitors to our Tuesday night prayer meetings get inspired and want to go and do likewise back home. But it is very important to discern God's guidance as to the true spiritual temperature of a congregation and what the next step should be.

While some pastors have started prayer meetings similar to ours and have seen a wonderful response, others have been disappointed. Many times the spirit of prayer has been so absent in a church that a weeknight prayer meeting, no matter how biblical or laudable, meets with apathy and coldness. This discourages pastors even more, and they feel doubly defeated as fewer and fewer people come each week.

I often recommend that these pastors adjust the Sunday service instead. Preaching time can be shortened somewhat, and when the sermon is over, invite those who feel touched by the Word to come forward for prayer. Get your staff and the church's spiritual leaders around you and pray with them. What is an "altar service"? It's a mini prayer meeting.

After people find more freedom to bring their needs to God, the spirit of prayer can begin to take hold. Then God will lead you to the next step. We must always remember that prayer is a gift from the Holy Spirit, and we can't work it up. So give God time to work in people's hearts. After they have experienced the joy and power of his presence, God will be able to do even greater things.

4. Let us never accept the excuse that God cannot work in *our* situation . . . that our particular people are too rich, or too poor . . . too inner-city or too suburban . . . too traditional or too avant-garde. This kind of thinking is never found in the Word of God. No matter what ethnic origin or geogra-

phy characterizes the local church, we *can* see God do things just as he did in the book of Acts, since he has *never* changed. The only changing that can occur is within us.

Let us purpose in our hearts to change in his direction and see him do incredible things to the praise of the glory of his grace.

Notes

Chapter Two—Catching Fire

1. Tom Carter, comp., *Spurgeon at His Best* (Grand Rapids: Baker, 1988), p. 155: selections from the 1873 edition of the *Metropolitan Tabernacle Pulpit*, p. 218.

2. Andrew A. Bonar, *Heavenly Springs* (Carlisle, PA: Banner of Truth Trust, 1904), p. 15.

Chapter Four—The Greatest Discovery of All Time

1. Tom Carter, comp., *Spurgeon at His Best* (Grand Rapids: Baker, 1988), p. 145: selections from the 1901 edition of the *Metropolitan Tabernacle Pulpit*, p. 247.

2. Copyright © 1989 Carol Joy Music\ASCAP (admin. ICG)\Word Music\ASCAP. All rights reserved. Used by permission.

Chapter Five—The Day Jesus Got Mad

1. J. B. Phillips, *The Young Church in Action* (New York: Macmillan, 1955), p. vii.

2. Ibid., p. viii.

3. Lyle Wesley Dorsett, *E. M. Bounds, Man of Prayer* (Grand Rapids: Zondervan, 1991), p. 134.

Chapter Six—A Time for Shaking

1. Andrew A. Bonar, *Heavenly Springs* (Carlisle, PA: Banner of Truth Trust, 1904), p. 34.

Chapter Seven—The Lure of Novelty

1. Cited in V. Raymond Edman, *They Found the Secret* (Grand Rapids: Zondervan, 1984), p. 46.

Chapter Eight—The Lure of Marketing

1. Marc Spiegler, "Scouting for Souls," *American Demographics* (March 1996), pp. 42–49.

Chapter Nine—The Lure of Doctrine Without Power

1. William Law, *The Power of the Spirit* (Fort Washington, PA: Christian Literature Crusade, 1971), p. 19.
2. Ibid., p. 124.
3. E. M. Bounds, *Powerful and Prayerful Pulpits* (Grand Rapids: Baker, 1993), p. 55.
4. J. Edwin Orr, *America's Great Revival* (Elizabethtown, PA: McBeth Press, 1957), p.11.
5. Quoted by Wendy Murray Zoba, "Father, Son, and . . . ," *Christianity Today* (June 17, 1996), p. 21.
6. Law, *The Power of the Spirit*, p. 23.

Chapter Eleven—In Search of Ordinary Heroes

1. Cited by J. Paul Reno, *Daniel Nash: Prevailing Prince of Prayer* (Asheville, NC: Revival Literature, 1989), p. 8.
2. For a fuller account of this event, see Garth M. Rosell and Richard A. G. Dupuis, eds., *The Memoirs of Charles G. Finney: The Complete Restored Text* (Grand Rapids: Zondervan, 1989), pp. 119–20.
3. Reno, *Daniel Nash*, p. 160.

Fresh Faith

JIM CYMBALA
WITH DEAN MERRILL

What Happens When Real Faith Ignites God's People

In an era laced with worry about the present and cynicism about the future, in a climate in which we've grown tired of hoping for miracles and wary of trumped-up claims that only disappoint, comes a confident reminder that God has not fallen asleep. He has not forgotten his people nor retreated into semi-retirement. On the contrary, he is ready to respond to real faith wherever he finds it.

Pastor Jim Cymbala insists that authentic, biblical faith is simple, honest, and utterly dependent upon God, a faith capable of transforming your life, your church, and the nation itself.

Jim Cymbala calls us back to the authentic, biblical faith, a fiery, passionate preoccupation with God that will restore what the enemy has stolen from us: our first love for Jesus, our zeal, our troubled children, our wounded marriages, our broken and divided churches. Born out of the heart and soul of The Brooklyn Tabernacle, the message of *Fresh Faith* is illustrated by true stories of men and women whose lives have been changed through the power of faith.

Hardcover 0-310-23007-1
Audio Pages 0-310-23006-3

We want to hear from you. Please send your comments about this
book to us in care of the address below. Thank you.

ZondervanPublishingHouse
Grand Rapids, Michigan 49530
http://www.zondervan.com